Your dog's senses

Your dog's senses

By Dr. Brigitte Rauth-Widmann

Copyright © of original edition 2005 by Cadmos GmbH, Brunsbek
Copyright © of this edition 2006 by Cadmos Equestrian
Translated by: Jennifer Schermer
Typesetting and design: Ravenstein + Partner, Verden
Photos: Karl-Heinz Widmann
Printers: Westermann Druck, Zwickau

Printed in Germany

ISBN 978-3-86127-923-5

For Ralf

"In particular, those who love animals and are trying to understand them have to expect them to probably experience the world completely differently to how we do. Those who, right from the beginning, read human feelings into their behaviour or even regard them as "better humans" don't do them justice. That understanding for animals turns into a misunderstanding."

Volker Arzt and Immanuel Birmelin

Contents

Preface

The dog is considered to be man's best friend, but what do we actually know about its sense organs and its perception? There is a lot written about the dog's body language, equally about its appropriate socialisation, upbringing and training. The required anatomical and physiological requirements for successful communication and interaction haven't really been cleared up though.

In the following book about the fascinating sensory perceptions of our four-legged friends, we are intending to close this gap – hopefully without proposing miraculous powers. For the precise adjustments and the excellent sensitivity of its natural senses are simply sufficient for the dog to be able to achieve incomparable performances. Certainly, they don't manage to do everything from birth. Some of the sense organs are not even sufficiently developed at that early stage to fulfil their function; furthermore those senses that are already working are still mainly underdeveloped, so that they can only give the little puppies a less differentiated picture of the world around them.

But with every hour, every day, the growth and maturing processes of the puppies' sensual system proceeds and along with it, the complexity and the acuteness of their senses grow unstoppably.

Witness how newborn puppies perceive the world around them and how the sense organs develop as time goes by and their sensibility finally reaches its peak. Join us on a journey through the "dog's sensual channels" and experience how dogs feel, smell and taste, how they see and how they hear and how they benefit from their sound sense of equilibrium.

The development
of the puppy's senses

Enormous powers are pressing it through a bottleneck. Suddenly the heavy pressure on its little body stops and the newborn puppy feels coldness and an unfamiliar sense of space around it. This unedifying experience nevertheless only lasts for a moment until something wet and warm is run over its skin and its still sparse hair. Literally shaken up through the licking movements, at that moment the tiny puppy has nothing else in mind than aspiring to the big comforting source of heat it is feeling right next to it.

Still quite uncoordinated, paddling with its short front legs, it crawls straight up to its mother's belly: the closer it comes, the faster it gets. Right at the teats, that are now optimally supplied with blood, it digs itself into its mother's fur and moves its mighty little head, trembling, from one side to the other, until its lips come across a firm mastoid elevation.

The newborn has several tiny warts on the front third of its tongue, the so-called lingual papillae. They help make things airtight while the puppy is drinking. As the the puppy gets older the papillae become fewer until they disappear completely after weaning.

Ambitiously, it now opens its little mouth (that really seems to be huge compared to the rest of its body), sticks out its cherry-red tongue and with it encloses the reward for its efforts: the elixir dispensing drug of its mother.

It does this so tightly and firmly that it creates an actual vacuum – that is clearly audible as a distinctive "plop" when it is unintentionally separated from the milk stream. At the same time, the puppy plants its strong front paws against the bitch's teats and kneads busily. A pleasurable smacking sound is soon heard – not only when you prick your ears!

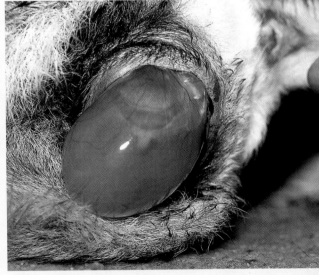

During the passage through the vulva, the puppy is still surrounded by the amniotic sac. Besides the tiny little nose and the left front paw you can already clearly see its distinctive tongue.

Development of the dog's senses

Sense	Beginning of perception	Maximum sensitivity
Touch through pressure, touch or vibration receptors of the skin (sense of touch, tactile perception, mechanoreception)	In the uterus, before the birth	A few days after birth – apart from, for example, the touch receptors of the paw pads, that probably reach their maximum perceptiveness after several weeks
Temperature registration through cold and warmth receptors of the skin (thermoreception)	In the uterus	A few days after birth
Perception of pain through pain receptors (nociception)	In the uterus	A few days after birth
Identification of the position in space through equilibrium organs in the inner ear (equilibrium or balance sense)	In the uterus	A few days after birth
Perception of smells through the vomeronasal organ at the palate (sense of smell or olfactory sense)	Probably already in the uterus, at the latest right after birth	With sexual maturity
Smell through the olfactory sensory cells of the regio olfactoria in the nose (sense of smell or olfactory sense)	Several scent components of fleeting scents can already be perceived a few hours after birth	Continuous increase of performance, the olfactory epithelium is fully developed by the end of the 4th - 5th month – refinement of differentiation of odorous substances is possible throughout life
Taste through taste buds of the tongue (sense of taste, gustatory sense)	Probably already in the uterus	A few days after birth
Vision through photoreceptors of the retina (visual sense, optic sense)	At about 14 days	At the age of 2 to 3 months
Hearing through the hearing organ (organ of Corti) in the inner ear (hearing sense, acoustic sense)	Through the ears at about 17 days – whether there is some kind of hearing experience through vibration and bone conduction, even before birth, seems to be questionable because of the underdevelopment of the hearing cells	At the age of about 3 months

What newborns can already perceive

A puppy is a strictly tactile animal – that's what people say – but it is not really correct. Newborn puppies do not only orientate themselves through tactile impulses. They do so also with the aid of other senses, because both the equilibrium sense of the puppies' inner ear and the numberless thermo receptors of their skin, as well as the pain perceiving sensory cells, have already started working – even if only to a restricted extent. All those senses were already awakening during growth in the uterus.

That is how the foetus of a dog can already register different environmental stimuli, like pressure and vibration, inside their wet homes. At especially sensitive body regions like lips, eyes, tongue and nasal plane, they can feel pain, too, as the receptors for this special sense, the so-called nociceptors, are remarkably numerous and well developed in these regions. The puppies also already react clearly to changes in temperature. Cold impulses, for example, cause increased body and extremity movements that resemble defence behaviour in foetuses from about seven weeks old. Warmth and gentle swaying, in contrast, lead to a relaxed body posture and a reduction of their pulse rates. The newborns can also definitely feel the swinging movements of their mother, as their equilibrium organ is already well developed and functioning by the middle of pregnancy. Based on this knowledge, it is not surprising that prenatal sensual experiences significantly affect the development of the puppy.

It's not only the state of health and the proper supply of nutrients to the pregnant bitch that contribute to the healthy development of her offspring. As her unborn puppies' senses are already awakening during this period, and the small puppies perceive varied stimuli and keep them in mind, the bitch should additionally be kept in a harmonic atmosphere and provided with lots of stroking, so that she gives birth to well-adjusted and flexible babies.

In contrast, other sense organs, like for example the eyes, are still quite underdeveloped, even when the puppy is born. They are not fully functioning until some weeks later. Furthermore their nerve tracts that lead to the brain only get connected little by little, so the absorbed optic impulses cannot get to higher areas of the central nervous system to be processed any earlier than that. Visual impressions therefore don't play a role for the puppy, neither inside the uterus nor right after birth. However, temperature and touch do play a respective role, for example, in the awareness of its position in space. The puppy, that can't yet control its body temperature independently, can only get food and the ever so important warmth, if he is able to perceive information about where those two vital factors are. He also needs to be able, more or less purposefully, to address and reach those places as quickly as possible. An animal that can't orientate itself through its position in space, tumbles around but never advances properly.

Breeders will probably know this very well: if you turn a newborn puppy onto its back quickly, it immediately spreads out its

Sensory cells that react automatically are notably numerous in the dog's facial area, especially on its nasal plane. There are also quite a lot of thermoreceptors in the dog's face, and some of them, on the tiny little nose, even seem to be susceptible to infrared radiation.

With its eyes and auditory canals still firmly closed, this three-day old Kelpie puppy is having a rest from suckling. It doesn't seem to be having feelings of hunger that are communicated through a number of specific receptors inside the body, although its mouth seems to be dreaming of the next tasty meal.

front and back legs. This inherent behaviour, the so-called Moro-reaction, allows the tiny puppy to orientate itself in space and, if necessary, to stabilise itself according to gravity, when it loses its position. If this typical reflex is missing or is only weakly developed, this is an indication of dysfunction, especially of the equilibrium sense. As with humans, this behaviour is already shown in the uterus.

About sensory cells and neurons

Nerve cells (neurons) have a cell body, the soma, and one or more tree-shaped appendices, the dendrites. With the latter, they can pick up signals coming from other cells and transmit them to their own soma. Furthermore nerve cells have a single very big appendix, the axon, that sends information from its own soma to other nerve cells. Thus every single nerve cell acts both as a signal receiver and as a signal transmitter within a huge system, the nervous system.

Sensory cells can be imagined as transformed nerve cells, whose appendices have turned into stimuli receivers, and thus work as receptors for sensory stimuli. Due to their construction and their connection, there are three different types:

- The primary sensory cell: this receives stimuli with its sensible cell appendices. The triggered nervous impulses are transmitted to the central nervous system through the axon of the same cells (for example, olfactory sensory cells, several touch receptors)
- The sensory nerve cell: this cell body doesn't lie in a thick layer of cells, the so-called epithelium, but is located at, or in, the central nervous system. The stimuli receiving end fibres are – as so-called free nerve endings – often strongly ramified (for example cold, warmth and pain receptors) or have special structures, like for instance tactile corpuscles (for example several touch receptors of the skin).

- The secondary sensory cell: this is always lying in an epithelium, doesn't have its own axon and only works as a stimuli receiver. It transmits its stimulation – through so-called synapses (see below) – to one of the surrounding ramified fibres of an attaching nerve cell (for example hair cells of the hearing and equilibrium organs, gustatory sensory cells, light receptors).

As the information from the environment reaches the body in different ways (with optic stimuli, we have electromagnetic waves or light quantum; with touch stimuli, mechanic energy, and so on) it needs stimuli specific sensory cells (receptors). At adequate power of a certain stimulus, the specific receptor will only be stimulated by its correct stimulator. Only if the intensity of the stimulus is extraordinarily high can receptors, that are usually not responding to such a kind of stimulus, also be stimulated: a heavy mechanic stimulus on the eye, for instance a punch in the face, can cause certain optic impressions.

Thus it is assured that only a single channel of information transmits announcements to the central nervous system concerning a very special kind of stimulus, as a decoding of different modalities cannot be undertaken any more on a higher level. Complex parameters of the information are worked out here instead, by comparing and modifying the stimulation patterns of many different sensory cells with each other.

How is information transmitted from the receptor cell to the brain?

Whatever type of receptor we are looking at, the arrival of an adequate stimulus always leads to a change in the membrane quality. This again leads to the development of a receptor potential, therefore to a local answer. The stronger the stimulus is, the higher the receptor potential gets.

If the relative threshold is exceeded through sufficient strength of the stimulus, an action potential is triggered, which not only stays at its point of development – like the receptor potential – but is also transferred through the nerve tract. The stronger the stimulus the more often such an action potential can be triggered. The information about the strength of the stimulus, received by the receptor, is now encoded as the rate of the action potential (impulses per second). A weak stimulus triggers only few nerve impulses per unit of time, a strong one, however, triggers many of them.

Because of the membrane quality of the axons, action potentials can be triggered again and again at entire amplitude. If this wasn't the case, electric impulses would quickly ebb away because of the high resistor of the nerve fibres. Thus the signals are refreshed constantly and can even reach a goal that is meters away at full level.

For a signal to be transmitted from one nerve fibre to the other (but also to muscles or glands) chemical messengers are usually required. Most of the time, even with nerve fibres crowded together, the distances are too big to be overcome just electrically. The special point of contact for such a chemical transmission is called synapse; the chemical substances are called neurotransmitters. The synaptic transmission works as follows:

As soon as the travelling stimulation in a nerve fibre reaches a switch point, the synapse, the neurotransmitters are released from little vesicles. The neurotransmitters then diffuse across the tiny space between the nerve cells, the synaptic cleft, and bind to special receptors of the nerve fibre. The chemical stimulus thereby arising is now the signal for the nerve fibre to emit electric impulses. The transmission of the stimulus is therefore ensured.

The number of molecules being released at a synapse depends on the strength of the local extent of stimulation – in this case, the rate of the action potential. The higher the rate, the more transmitter molecules are released. And the more molecules bind up to the receptor cell, the stronger is the triggered effect.

Feeling pain is vital

What the puppy needs furthermore, on its journey to the life-saving source of food and warmth, is a feeling for painful experiences. A long-lasting contact with a tissue damaging stimulus (for example a sharp needle or burning hot obstacle) is to be avoided by all means. As probably expected, nature has already equipped newborns with fully functioning pain receptors that trigger either avoidance reactions or cause them to utter cries of pain, or at least discomfort when stimulated, which in turn immediately alarms the mother (or the human caretaker).

Against all contrary observations, dogs, even the youngest among them, can feel painful stimuli along their whole body. How strongly they perceive them depends – besides the intensity of the stimulus – on the region of the body where those excessively strong mechanical or chemical stimuli appear. The animal's legs are least sensitive to pain; most sensitive are the face and the stomach, as well as the testicles. This is due to the different number of pain receptors in these areas. An especially large number of pain receptors are situated in the oral cavity, on the tongue, along the lips and on the skin of the dog's nose, as well as around its eyes. The touch receptors, which react to touch, pressure and vibration, and the temperature sensors of the dog's skin, the warmth and cold receptors, are similarly spread.

As the dog's pain system is structured and works just as ours does, dogs probably perceive pain in the same way as we do, and

An especially large number of pain receptors are situated in the facial area. When these areas are additionally sore, they hurt even more. This is caused by chemical substances that, due to the inflammation, are released by the affected cells. They enhance the sensitivity of the pain receptors and alert them to pain.

might even suffer accordingly. Dogs, however, have altogether less pain receptors on their skin (in contrast to the inside of their body) than we do. Furthermore they usually have a protecting fur that defends them against all kinds of harmful influences that could cause pain. Nevertheless, at the most sensitive areas of their body, usually even minor stimuli can cause heavy pain reactions. They result, for example, in an increase of the breathing rate, the pulse rate and the blood pressure – whether it's a puppy or an older dog (just as in humans).

A thick coat of hair protects against injury better than a sparser one, but it also very warm and requires certain behavioural reactions, such as moving less or resting in the shade, when it is hot.

To what extent those changes happen, depends on extremely different tolerance limits. The physical symptoms of pain are also very different in every individual. Often the behaviour pattern, especially in older dogs, is influenced by previous experiences they have had: thus one becomes remarkably calm, another aggressive; one dog expresses screams of pain, another whines, whimpers or sighs; yet another will constantly grind its teeth. Some animals tremble and pant heavily when they are in pain, others only react with accelerated breathing; some of them snuggle up to their owners, others avoid them.

However the dog reacts, such drastic behavioural changes of habits should never be ignored. Instead this should be the reason for any dog owner to start searching for the cause. The dog's life could depend on it.

When a living being is vexed with pain, there is always a good reason. Pain is a warning signal of the body given to the ap-perception in order to make it do something to stop this bad feeling and at the same time also to stop the trigger. If our dog is not able to take countermeasures itself, we have to take this task over for him and take him to the vets quickly, for example!

When the cause of the pain is identified and a proper treatment is initiated, one should neither feel sorry for the dog nor comfort it. For example, trying to distract it from its bad feelings with appropriate occu-pation is much better for its well-being and a quick recovery.

Pain receptors don't adapt, which means that they don't get used to their triggers, and, like many other receptors, only react extenuated for a while. When current pain is suddenly perceived as less strong, it is because inhibit-ing interactions on a higher level temporarily weaken the impulse transition to the nerve tracts, that, for example, lead to the cerebral cortex (and therewith to consciousness).

When chronic diseases, such as joint dys-plasia, cause the pain, distraction usually doesn't help much. Often, in this case, be-sides physiotherapy, only painkillers can bring real relief. Unfortunately, the big joints of the dog, in particular, contain a remark-ably high number of pain receptors, so that defects cause exceptionally high discomfort there.

Highly sensitive tactile sensors

The senses of touch, temperature and pain are not confined to special sense organs, as for instance the visual sense is confined to the eyes. Mechanical, thermal and pain stim-uli can be perceived by the dog anywhere in and on its body. It only requires suitable sen-sory cells that register and transfer those stimuli: the receptors. There is a vast num-ber of them, both on the surface of its body (skin sensibility) and inside its body, such as in the joints and the inner organs (proprio-ception and intestinal sensitivity). The touch sensitive ones are measuring, for instance, the current blood pressure, the gastro-intes-tinal dilatation or the position of the joints and the length of the muscles there.

At this point we will only be looking at the receptors of the dog's skin. Usually this in-volves the so-called free nerve endings– all next to each other and in varying concentra-tion – that are spread out over the whole body: a huge system of microscopic tactile corpuscles that equip the skin with an excel-lent sense of touch.

Dogs have the highest perception on their nose leather. Here the tactile corpuscles stand especially close beside each other. The skin of the nose leather, that is clear of hair and glands and usually darkly pigmented, shows wrinkles that result in a typical pattern. This pattern dif-fers so clearly from animal to animal that it can even act as an individual feature, just as the hu-man fingerprint. On both sides of the so-called philtrum (this is the centrally located distinc-tive wrinkle of the nose leather, beginning at the level of the nostrils), as well as where nose leather and upper lip blend into each other, there

The door to the most impressive sensual organ of the dog is extremely touch, temperature and pain sensitive and also contains its most important acupressure point.

seems to exist a different skin resistance than at the surrounding tissue.

This fact points to the existence of acupuncture points. Actually, smart dog owners and vets are already using this "emergency point" by stimulating it with strong thumb pressure (for instance in cases of an imminent circulatory failure) – the easiest form of acupressure.

The canine tactile perception is not only of particular importance during puppy hood but also later on, for instance, when communicating with other dogs.

Whether dogs are showing submissive or dominant behaviour, there is almost always some kind of tactile interaction happening, for instance in terms of social grooming, licking the corners of the mouth, lying next to each other and also when pushing each other away or placing the head on the other's back.

Tactile perception

There are three different types of mechanoreceptors:

- Pressure or strength detectors – they react to pressure; the stronger the pressure the higher the impulse rate of the electric information sent to the brain.
- Touch or tempo detectors – they react to touch, whereas it is not so much the intensity of the touch but the speed with which the stimulus is happening. The faster the stimulation happens the higher the impulse rate.
- Vibration or acceleration detectors – they only react persistently when the speed of the stimulus is varying constantly. The impulse rate then is in proportion to the acceleration.

As dogs are especially touch sensitive around the whole head area, they respond very well to caressing or massage there. Early body contact is important for a healthy development – psychologically as well as physiologically.

Temperature perception

There are two different types of thermoreceptors:

- Cold receptors – they are stimulated by coldness; the lower the temperature, the higher the impulse rate at the deriving nerve fibres.
- Warmth receptors – they are stimulated by warmth; the higher the temperature, the higher the impulse rate at the deriving nerve fibres.

The strenuous licking of the mother in the anal area triggers the urogenital reflex through special touch receptors which causes the puppy to defecate and urinate; without this stimulation he would not be able to do so yet.

Even when one of its tactile hairs on the forehead is lightly touched, the dog closes its lids – a defence reflex.

Vibrissae are well-built; their hair root receptors are extremely sensitive. Even these special hairs come out regularly and grow again. This, however, happens completely independent of the dog's normal seasonal fur change.

Whiskers for orientation

It is not only the dog's skin surface that is extremely sensitive. At the base of every single one of the millions of hairs – as well as the eyelashes (that dogs only have along the upper eyelid) – there are touch receptors. Each tiny hair is covered with such nerve fibres at its root that turn it into a kind of touch receptor.

The so-called whiskers, that are especially plentiful in the dog's face, are of course especially sensitive. As vibrissae, they surround the nose and mouth area; as tactile hairs, they grow around the eyes and on the forehead.

The dog can assess the wind direction with the aid of its temperature receptors on its nose leather.
The vibrissae register the finest airstreams, especially.

Furthermore, several whiskers are to be found scattered over the dog's whole body – they are called guard hairs. All of those hairs are already well developed at the puppy's birth, which shows how important they are.

Whiskers are modified hairs that are longer, more rigid and fixed much deeper into the skin. The netting of nerve fibres around their roots is denser and it includes the blood-filled follicle, the so-called blood sinus (by which every whisker is surrounded at its basis). This special anatomical construction particularly aids the record of stimuli. The movements caused by touching such a strong hair first generate a vibration of the blood liquid at its base. Then, clearly reinforced, they reach the sensitive free nerve endings.

Besides the direction and the intensity with which the hair is bent, at the same time those special sensors register at what speed it was bent. Because of their extraordinarily high sensitivity, they even register the finest variations in air pressure and air eddies. Thus, even without being touched, whiskers can register obstacles and help their four-legged bearers to orientate themselves.

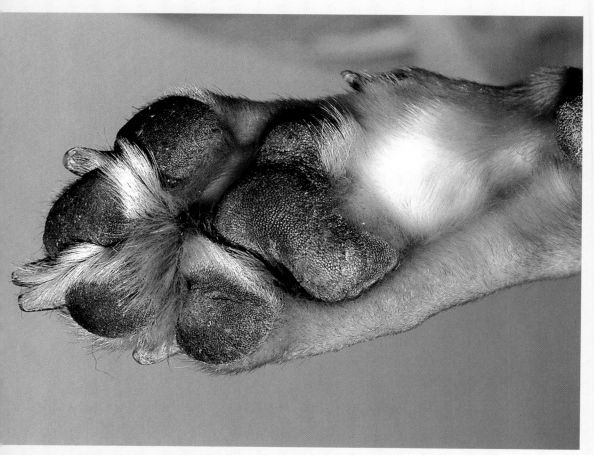

The dog's paw pads are extremely sensitive, especially to vibration. This fine perceptive faculty develops within the first few weeks of the puppy's life – newborns' paws are still sending quite undifferentiated signals to the brain.

Touch sensors at the paws

From your biology classes, do you remember the seemingly malformed "cortex-man" (related to the cerebral cortex), whose parts of the body were illustrated with deformed proportions, according to their representation in the brain? With dogs, it is similar, as all tactile information from its body surface gathers in the cerebral cortex and results in an exact topographic picture of its perceptive faculty. Parts of the body where the dog is especially sensitive take up the biggest space. This is why the animal, head – and mainly the nose, the lips and the tongue – is reproduced oversized, as well as its paws, which are also among the strongly touch-sensitive parts of the body. This is due to the infinite tiny nerve structures, the so-called Pacinian corpuscles, which are situated right under the surface of the paw pads.

Only about 1mm insize, consisting of a large number of concentric lamellae, and filled with cell fluid, those seismographic fine touch sensors register any tiny vibration, while treading carefully and give the dog the most exact information about what is going on in the ground.

Inside the lamellae, such vibrations cause fractional changes in pressure that are transferred to the nerve fibres inside the receptor and finally to the brain. Dogs even perceive the vibration of the ground caused by our steps, mainly through their sensitive paw pads.

Touch sensors and free nerve endings are not only situated in the dog's paw pads but also at the base of its claws. Furthermore, the carpal pad (situated at the level of the carpal bones) is well-stocked with them: another sensitive touch receptor that helps the dog to get along safely in pathless areas.

Smelling and tasting

With the perception of touch, pressure and vibration, the registration of warmth and coldness, as well as the sense of pain, the perceptive faculty of a newborn puppy is nowhere near complete. Newborn babies can also identify several smells and tastes quite clearly.

Even a foetus can probably perceive certain smells and tastes, when it swallows a few drops of the amniotic fluid during its development in the uterus, that it recognises as familiar later on. However there is no scientific proof. But presumably, whatever the mother eats during pregnancy, and what shows up as smell (olfactory) and taste (gustatory) in the amniotic fluid as well as in the milk, turns into a calming "key stimulus" for the puppies.

The registration of taste in the womb is easy to imagine – namely through the tongue.

It is, however, doubtful how an unborn mammal that, as it's generally known, takes its first breath after passing through the birth canal, can experience an olfactory perception. There probably is an easy explanation for that, which nobody has thought of yet: the vomeronasal organ (VNO), a sort of oral olfactory organ that works in puppies nearly as well as in adult dogs.

The mysterious VNO

This tubular entity, a few millimetres thick, and also called Jacobson's organ after its discoverer the Danish doctor Jacobson, is situated right at the dog's nasal septum, on the edge of the nasal cavity. Compared to other mammals that have such an additional smelling organ, in dogs this usually quite plain, dead end tube has irregular wrinkles. Furthermore, it is clearly longer (5 to 6 centimetres) than in many other animals, and runs from the incisors back to the first or second premolar. X-rays have shown that shape and relative length are breed-specific, whereas both factors are closely linked to the animal's skull proportions.

Just as the sensitive nose (see page 28), the dog's olfactory sense organ has a thick olfactory epithelium on its inner surface, whose sensory cells contain hundreds of small hairs. These hairs, which are probably directly concerned in the processing of olfactory stimuli, seem to be unique in dogs. They are not only numerous, but also very tender and flexible. In all other animal groups that have been examined regarding this, the receptor cells of this organ only showed several standing

*Who would have though the roof of the dog's mouth concealed a smelling organ
so sensitive it can pick up scents that the nose doesen't even respond to.*

rigid bristles. This is also an indication that the dog's vomeronasal organ is especially sensitive.

But where does it get its information from? There is no direct link to the actual olfactory epithelium of the nose but – through a small corridor in the roof of the oral cavity – to the oral cavity. Accordingly the vomeronasal organ receives its information through two gateways: the airspace in the nose and the mouth opening. Interestingly the olfactory sense organ is almost not responsive to volatile scents that are exclusively provided through the nose. The heavy non-volatile odorous sub-

stances from the oral cavity (and the nose) are the ones that cause significant reactions in the sensory cells.

It is these prominent scent molecules that come from a very special source, the so-called pheromones that other dogs excrete with their body fluids. These messengers, that are similar to hormones, are characteristically only effective and understood between members of the same species and therefore, they only trigger defined reactions in members of the same type, such as elements of sexual behaviour.

Presumably, specific pheromone precursors are already active within the body, for instance when they get into the amniotic fluid and therefore into the foetus' mouth through the uterus; although these important olfactory informants are usually found in the dog's faeces, the urine and the vaginal lubrication. Those species-specific odours can also be scented on dead hair particles and lost bushes of hair.

When the scent molecules can be directly licked off the body of the opposite sex, for instance a female in heat, the resulting changes in the recipient's metabolism and behaviour are most significant.

By the way, the animals aren't aware of exactly which fascinating smells they receive or that they have such a profound effect on them, as their signals simply by-pass the corresponding brain structures. The axons coming from the sensory cells of the vomeronasal organ are leading towards the olfactory bulb and are probably the most important scent processing centre in the dog's telencephalon. However they don't flow into the actual clubbed bulb – such as those coming from the olfactory epithelium of the nose – but into another structure, the accessory olfactory bulb. The latter is neither connected to the olfactory bulb itself nor to the cerebral cortex, which

means that incoming olfactory stimuli are not perceived deliberately by the animal (other than most of those coming from the nose). Instead the accessory olfactory bulb is almost exclusively in contact with the hypothalamus and the limbic system, brain structures that mainly control so-called autonomic bodily functions. These are, among others, the temperature regulation and ingestion, sexual behaviour and emotions.

Calm breathing through the nose is usually not enough to stimulate the vomeronasal organ to its maximum. To take in as many scent molecules as possible, the dog has to sniff thoroughly or, for example, lick. Only in this way can the appropriate scent molecules arrive on its tongue and also on the oral mucosa in a sufficient number, from where they are moved further together with the plentiful secreted saliva to the hard palate with its passage to the VNO. This can also be achieved through pressing the tongue against the roof of the oral cavity. Pumping movements of the vomeronasal organ quicken the exchange of liquids. In contrast to the actual smelling organ, the vomeronasal organ is not mainly filled with air, but with mucus.

Naturally, he can smell a bitch in heat 3 kilometres away. The higher the progesterone level in her excretions, the stronger his arousal.

When a sexually mature male perceives the smell of a female in heat, the use of his vomeronasal organ is clearly visible: He puts on a strange concentrated look, audibly sucks in the air through his mouth, trembles with his jaws and licks into the air. The result is that he usually ends up slobbering strongly and making smacking sounds. You may also hear a kind of cackling sound when he moves his head lightly from one side to other to check the surrounding air.

Two olfactory systems

Currently accepted opinion states that dogs have two separated olfactory systems that work in parallel and complement each other functionally. The main task of the olfactory epithelium of their nose is analysing different smells – even the ones of unknown origin and without social significance. However, it is presumed that the vomeronasal organ reacts to a rather genetically pre-programmed range of smells and especially identifies those smells that deliver differentiated information on sex, reproductive status and social rank.

The relevance of smells for puppies

Even unborn puppies probably register smells through the vomeronasal organ. At the latest, newborn puppies do so for sure, as this is the only explanation for why specific smells that only females release during confinement, cause significant behavioural changes in their offspring.

As many other mammal mothers, canine females produce a certain smell (non-perceivable for us humans) right after childbirth, and until the puppies are weaned this has a remarkably soothing effect on their babies. It consists of very simple, but rather large molecules. Tiny components therein make it species-specific and distinctive for the newborn puppies.

Because of its protection, conciliating and stress reducing effect, this special smell is

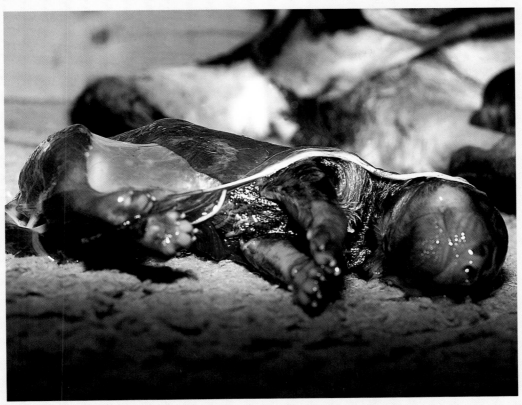

Yes, being born is stressful and it is cold as well. Its optimally developed senses of touch, temperature and equilibrium will show the puppy, just a few-minutes old, the quickest way to its mother's warming belly.

called the "appeasing pheromone", or in the dog's special case, the "dog appeasing pheromone" (DAP).

By the way, it not only has a calming effect on puppies, even adult dogs relax visibly when their surroundings are sprayed with this pheromone. In behavioural therapy for fearful dogs, DAP is applied successfully. (Several species-specific appeasing pheromones are available over the internet at present – they are supplied in a diffuser.) The female herself gives off her appeasing pheromones along the centre line of her belly, between the mammary glands, and therefore in a region where it flows directly into the puppies mouths.

The mammary glands close to the tail show higher metabolic activity and produce more milk than the ones closer to the breast. Thus they probably also give off more pheromones and other scents – besides more warmth. Anyhow, the puppies preferably seek out those teats. But only the stronger puppies of the litter manage to permanently occupy them. The weaker ones usually have to do with the less productive teats in the front. So it is up to the breeder to help his weaker puppies to suckle at the teats at the back.

The appeasing pheromone has obviously brought about an effect in this puppy.

The VNO in humans

Even we are remotely controlled and manipulated by scents in this way. We also have an additional olfactory system, even up to an old age. Once, it was assumed that the human vomeronasal organ would regress during adult age, but today we know better: Two tiny spots are situated on both sides of the nasal septum, about 1.5 centimetres above the nostrils (and you'll be sorry to lose them during cosmetic surgery!). These are also analyses pheromones and they are quite effective.

So it's not surprising that there are some people that we just can't stand and others whose smell we quite like. We don't need to activate some kind of sixth sense for that. However, human pheromones have a significantly lower range than dog's. Our hormonal messengers often only work with close body contact. Of course, human mothers also produce a species-specific appeasing pheromone to calm down their offspring – it is expediently given off around the areola.

Can newborns perceive smells with their nose? With its first, deep breath the newborn puppy absorbs the whole olfactory spectrum of its close surroundings. As this happens, the infinite number of scent molecules of the incoming air skim along the actual olfactory receptors of its posterior nasal cavity. Whether these cells are already in a position to perceive these mainly fleeting molecules as adequate stimuli, and to what extent this is possible, has hardly been investigated scientifically. Today it is presumed that newborn puppies have an extremely restricted olfactory perception through their nose (compared with the one through their oral olfactory organ). This is also indicated by the hardly measurable electrical activity of the olfactory nerve fibres and the relatively underdeveloped correspondent olfactory centre in the brain.

Presumably, several scents can even be registered and identified by newborns. It seems to be mainly specific smells coming from the milk. Experiments with puppies a few days old have shown that the little babies can also definitely perceive neutral smells such as aniseed.

But during their first days of life, dogs are certainly not capable of such an impressing perception and distinction of smells as they will be in the future. Also the perceptive faculty of the vomeronasal sensory cells is nowhere near perfected – why should it be? As generally known, pheromones don't reach their full importance before sexual maturity.

Gustatory perception

When adult dogs use their vomeronasal organ, they don't do it in the same way as, for instance, horses do when flehming. Instead, they surprise us with this noticeable, loud, smacking and sniffing. This seems to point towards the fact that, besides the receptors of the oral olfactory organ, the ones on the tongue are also being deployed, as the dog's big muscular tongue, with its infinite number of touch receptors, is not just a very sensitive touch organ. Thanks to the plentiful gustatory cells in its mucous membrane, it is also responsible for the sense of taste. The saliva acts as solvent for the flavours.

Gustatory receptors are scattered along the dog's entire tongue. Mostly they are grouped into so-called taste buds that likewise are grouped into small verruciform gustatory papillae.

The number of taste buds is crucial for the gustatory perception. The more there are on the tongue, the more subtle is the perception. Thereby the number of buds is directly related to the chewing time spent by an animal. The longer a mammal moves its food around in its mouth while chewing, the more such chemically sensitive spots can be found on its tongue. Dogs, that tend to gulp down their food instead of chewing it, have around 1,700 taste buds on the mucous membrane of their tongue. By comparison, humans have roughly 9,000; cattle 25,000. It also turns out that animals that have an especially subtle olfactory capability only have a comparatively

Who said that dogs don't have preferences of taste?
They are simply not always similar to ours.

low gustatory perception and a rough ability to differentiate between different flavours – and vice versa.

As they also have different types of gustatory sensory cells that react to specific stimuli, dogs can, however, distinguish the four taste sensations: sweet, sour, bitter and salty. Unlike most other sensory cells, gustatory re-

ceptors react to several substances and also their forwarding nerve fibres show a so-called graded specificity. Thereby the thresholds for bitter and sweet sensations are especially low.

Dogs generally refuse bitter substances. If something bitter is accidentally eaten, together with other food, this usually results in choking or vomiting. The corresponding gustatory receptors therefore trigger an automatic protective mechanism. Sweet flavours, however, seem to be our dogs' favourites. As an important part of the food, sugar is also contained in especially high concentrations in, for instance, fresh grass shoots. That is probably the reason why they enjoy going for such tasty treats.

Dogs obviously can't quantify flavours very well: they can perceive whether a food contains salt, but not whether it is tastelessly seasoned, or whether it is over salted.

They are really also no gourmets! But they are way ahead of us when it comes to sensing the existence of water. Dogs have special chemical sensors on their tongue that only react to water. That means that such receptors can undoubtedly distinguish water from other liquids. How they manage to do so is still a miracle.

As with other senses, early gustatory and olfactory sensations are defining for a dog. The more restricted the food range of a dog is during its puppy hood, the more difficult changes of food will become, when it is an adult. Whether the gustatory perception varies according to the age – as in humans – is not known. But it is certain that puppies perceive distinctive gustatory sensations a few days after their birth.

Besides gustatory papillae, there are lots of little warts working automatically that also help to clean the coat. As gustatory and olfactory perception are closely related to each other, it is not surprising that the secretion of saliva starts as soon as a dog perceives the scent of food.

While dreaming, the puppy's brain is especially mentally active. The puppy also breathes more quickly and its heart beats faster.

In the land of dreams

Puppies need a lot of sleep – not only because they are not very demanding at this age and need a lot of rest periods, but also because the hormones needed for growth are released while sleeping.

Within their first two weeks of life, they nevertheless don't seem to be dreaming. This doesn't happen before the puppy's two last sensory organs – its eyes and ears – have started working. Then, suddenly, a lot of sensations reach the brain, which the puppy has to cope with while resting. It's only the so-called REM sleep (see right for explanation) that makes this possible. Its characteristic

brainwaves can be measured for the first time around the 20th day of life. From now on the puppies can dream. And they are now doing it very intensively and for long periods – much longer than they will when they are grown-ups. They dream less and less over the years. Senior dogs' dreams last less than 15 per cent of the whole sleeping time; in puppies, they last more than half of it.

During their dreams, dogs are smacking their lips, growling, barking and wagging their tails, moving their paws, twitching their legs and showing conspicuous facial expressions.

Furthermore, they exhibit REM: those typical movements of the eyes while sleeping, where the eyeballs move quickly in synchronisation from one side to the other, despite the eyelids being closed (REM stands for "rapid eye movement"). Constantly waking a dog up during those obviously exciting sleeping periods significantly affects its health. In puppies, a lack of REM sleeping periods can even cause development disorders as, according to a widely accepted theory, REM sleeping periods highly boost the brain growth – especially in very young dogs.

We would be only too pleased if we knew what dogs are actually experiencing when they are dreaming. Unfortunately we can't just ask them. It is assumed that they review previous experiences, digest them in that way and save them in their long-term memory.

Especially intense sensations during an active phase lead to intensified body movements during resting periods.

Although perception is clearly reduced while sleeping, the dog's sense organs are always alert, even when it is dreaming. Why not try it out one day? Hold a piece of attractively smelling food right in front of your dog's nose while it is dreaming. It will probably start sniffing, licking and maybe even smacking its lips, without really waking up. Only when it clearly perceives the smell for a longer period of time or when you touch it accidentally, will it perk up immediately.

The influence of sensory input on the development of the brain

Even as newborns, puppies perceive various details of their environment and react to things that happen to them. When, after 3-4 weeks, all of their sense organs are fully developed, they receive more and more unknown impressions to cope with. Second after second, the puppies are now learning new things (this is especially intensive during the so-called socialisation period, between the 4th and 12th weeks). The learning mechanism goes on forever.

Their strong reactions to environmental stimuli during this short period of life are conspicuous. They take immediate notice of unknown sounds, and unexpected optic impressions, that suddenly appear within their range of vision, make them wince briefly. But puppies at that age do not only react so strongly to optic, acoustic or olfactory impressions, but also to touch and social interactions. Why do they react so strongly to everything that is surrounding them at this age and more importantly, what for? Neurobiology gives us explanations.

Around the 25th day of life, something breathtaking that influences the rest of their life happens in puppies' brains: their infinite, widely scattered nerve cells, previously with only little connections to each other, stretch out their arms suddenly and start networking as quickly and closely as possible. Only when various connections between them are working, are the nerve cells able to take over the complex tasks that are now

When suitable sensory input is missing during a defined time slot, appropriate nerve connections can not be made and the central processing and assessment of the corresponding signals becomes impossible! The stimulation of even the smallest of puppies, therefore, becomes more important.

waiting for them and cope with them easily during the rest of their lives.

If they don't have those specific connections they cannot interact. The transfer of sensory input, or rather nerve impulses, wouldn't take place. The processing in the brain wouldn't happen, as well as a correct perception of sensations or an adapted behavioural response – a disastrous situation for any animal. The connection of nerve cells is not only taking place because the puppy

reaches a certain age. This differentiated process in its central nervous system also needs a trigger in the environment. For the development and networking of the nerve cells of its optic system, for instance, the trigger is light. This has to impinge on the retina of the puppy's eyes so that the cascade of connections starts.

At some point, a ray of light onto the retina is enough to make the system work – of course it's not that easy. The time frame within which the stimulus reaches the receptors is crucial to the normal process of development. In puppies, this has to be during those days when its eyelids open as tiny observation slits for the first time – therefore at the age of about two weeks.

When those light signals are missing during the period of eye opening, the development of synapses in the optical system fails to appear as, inevitably, does the correct processing and assessment of optical signals. Synaptic switch points can only be developed to a noteworthy extent when their so-called time slot is open. That means when exactly the lifespan that is genetically designated for the configuration of the processing of this special sensation, is reached. When there aren't any networking reactions within this period, most of the nerve cells in this processing complex become stunted or even die off completely, as they are apparently not needed.

For the auditory nerve cells, it's almost the same as the optical system, with the difference that they need acoustic stimuli instead of light to network in proper form. Sound reaches the receptors of the inner ear at sufficient strength for the first time when the puppy's ear canals break open at around 17 days and lets through the shock waves.

There is one more thing that contributes to the networking of nerve cells: the usage of those cells. The more often a certain nerve tract is used (as signals are transferred), the quicker, more often and more intensely, it links with other nerve fibres. The stronger the connection, the more efficient the brain, and the better equipped the whole organism.

Taking away all troubles from a puppy – even from the tiniest one – consequently doesn't have a favourable effect. For instance, when a puppy is always placed at the teats for drinking, instead of letting it crawl up to them by itself, there are effects on a level one wouldn't expect, namely on the development of its nerve tracts.

When a puppy is born, all its nerve fibres are virtually naked. During the first weeks of life – and as a result of signals, such as the movement of the extremities when crawling up to the teats – individual nerve fibres are covered by an isolating coat. The result: the nerve fibres can now transfer information much more quickly and better shielded from others. In this way, electric impulses get from one place to the other more quickly and more precisely. Thereby, the bundles of muscles fed by those nerves achieve a much higher reaction rate. The animal in question, therefore, has an improved ability of coordination.

Without those encouraging stimuli, the development of this so-called myelin sheath can be defective. This considerably affects the dog's motor faculties and therewith also its chances of survival.

Besides the physical efforts that puppies should make early on, even the temperature in their room or play area, for instance, has a significant effect on their healthy development. When puppies are always kept in an equally tempered environment (probably only cosy and warm), it does more harm to their health than good.

As even the ability to control the body temperature independently needs an impulse from outside. In this case, the impulse would

Mild stress, whether it is optical, acoustical, climatical, immunological or social stress, encourages the development of adjustment and regulation processes and increases the resilience of the whole animal.

be the contrast of different temperature signals, warmth as well as coldness – in moderate amounts of course!

When the ambient temperature is kept at the same level of warmth or when the puppies aren't allowed to go out, the starting signal for the differentiation process fails to appear. Consequently, those unfortunate dogs will always have significant difficulties in regulating their heat balance: a great deficit in the performance of their cardiovascular system.

Even the maturing, performance and reaction rate of their immune system are highly dependent on the conditions during their first weeks of growing up.

A world
full of smells

With his long, warm nose dipped deeply into the old slipper, Vitus absorbs the fragrance that comes out of it with downright devotional concentration. His owner Robert is even praising him for the strange behaviour that he displays in the middle of the marketplace. What's the point of that?

Pedestrians standing around watch curiously as the dog, in his tracking harness on the long leash and with his owner behind, sets off with determination along the pavement directly afterwards. First he sneaks along with his nose just above the pavement, sniffing with excitement at the kerbside.

A cigarette butt at the crime scene: was it thrown there by the suspect? The tracker dog working for the investigating agency sniffs at it and compares the scent picture gained with the scent of the potential delinquent. He can clarify the situation immediately. A DNA analysis takes much longer and also requires body material, the smell alone is not enough.

Next, he lifts his head up high and reads the olfactory information up in the air. He stops at a shopdoor, sure that the old man who, about two hours ago, announced his suicide has rushed along here.

But at the only bus station in town, he is thrown off the track. Vitus clearly shows Robert that he can't smell individual scent any more. Now they have to drive along the route and let the tracker dog check every bus station to see whether the missing person has left the bus. Every time, Vitus can sniff at the slipper Robert is carrying with him in a sealed plastic bag, so that he doesn't lose the memory of the individual scent pattern of the suicidal person.

Meanwhile. it has started to rain heavily. At the last bus station, Vitus finally absorbs the scent pattern he is searching for again. Eagerly he explores the direction in which the missing person has left. Faster and faster, he pulls forward. Suddenly, he begins to wag his tail and whines excitedly. There he is! Behind the bench at the pond squats the hopeless man, shaking and completely drenched; the two pillboxes that he is holding firmly in his clammy fingers are still completely full. Thanks to his sensationally fine and well-trained nose, Vitus has detected the old man early enough: a happy ending – at least for the moment.

From the nose leather to the olfactory bulb

It is certainly considered that the enormous number of olfactory sensory cells, as well as the type of connection with specific structures in the brain, are responsible for the high sensitivity of the dog's olfactory system and the lightening-fast detection of different smells in the slightest concentrations. However, the anatomical structure of the dog's nose itself is involved.

It is specially constructed, so that the inhaled air reaches the olfactory epithelium quite quickly and doesn't – as, for instance, in humans – have to travel a long way and thus consequently lose most of its olfactory information. Despite the short journey, the inhaled air is adequately warmed up and moistened, two important requirements for a good olfactory perception. A finely branching network of vessels in the mucous membrane of the dog's nose caters for an extraordinarily good blood flow; extremely efficient glands in the nose provide the continually necessary fluid. As a consequence of a good blood flow, there is a high evaporation rate of the secretion, which again leads to an increase of humidity inside the nose. In such a watery ambience, the gaseous scent molecules floating in the air dissolve easily and consequently get into extremely intense contact with the olfactory sensory cells in the back of the nasal cavity, the point of acceptance of this olfactory information.

In the dog's nose, there is also a precisely controlled mechanism of breathing in and out that regulates the strength of the air flowing through the nasal cavity and therewith the speed of the scent stream, and the amount of molecules skimming over the olfactory epithelium. Through intense sniffing, the speed rises up to 40 kilometres per hour – the amount of inhaled air increases from 6-60 litres of air per minute, compared to the normal breathing rate.

Real turbulence can arise through this kind of ventilation that additionally strengthens the transport of scent molecules to the olfactory

There is always a little fluid on the nose leather that either comes out of special glands in the nose or gets there by licking. The dog's typically cold nose occurs when this fluid film evaporates.

receptors and sensationally improves the olfactory performance.

The breathing capacity increases up to almost 75 litres per minute while panting, when the air stream goes not only through the nose, but also through the mouth. Such a breathing method, with up to 400 breaths per minute, helps evaporate liquid on the tongue and in the oral cavity and thus is more responsible for cooling down the body than improving the general perception of smells. Nevertheless, it is vital, as dogs cannot cool down their bodies by sweating – they simply don't have the necessary sweat glands in order to do that.

How does the dog's nose work?

The area for perception of transient scents is situated on the roof of the rear nasal cavity: the olfactory epithelium, also called regio olfactoria. It is covered with a thin layer of tissue and mucus that is made of three different types of cells: the olfactory receptor cells, the supporting cells and the basal cells. The basal cells develop into new olfactory nerve fibres as the dog's olfactory receptor cells only live for a very short period of not more than 30 days. (Our olfactory receptor cells evolve only every three months, which probably reflects the lower strain put on them.) The supporting cells contribute to the production of mucus in the rear nasal cavity and, at the same time, they act as electrical insulators that shield neighbouring olfactory nerve fibres from each other.

The olfactory epithelium contains about 200 million olfactory receptor cells, whose branches face the interior space of the nasal cavity from between the supporting cells and end in a button-like bulge. On top of each of those bulges, a tuft of 100 to 150 tiny 1 micrometer (=0.001 millimetres) long small

hairs protrude from the olfactory receptor cells' branches into the mucus, covering the surface of the olfactory epithelium and coming into direct contact with the air. These so-called olfactory cilia are the actual sensorial areas for the olfactory information – the average dog has at least 20 billion of them. In our olfactory epithelium, there are only about 5-10 million olfactory receptor cells, each with 5-20 of such cilia. We accordingly only have 25-200 million such hairs – and still our olfactory perception isn't too bad. So imagine how much more detailed and rich our dogs' perception must be.

But how do the scent molecules, dissolved in the mucus, come into contact with the olfactory cilia? Within the membrane of each cilium, special proteins, the so-called receptor proteins, can be found, to which the scent molecules have to connect before they can trigger a reaction. This reaction doesn't consist of, as is normal, the occurrence of a receptor potential. Inside the olfactory cilia, it at first comes to a chemical reaction, namely to a release of chemical messengers that result in an opening of the so-called ion channels inside its cell membrane. The ions that stream in, as a result, change the membrane potential, so that there is an electrical response. Due to these messengers, the olfactory receptor cell is able to react, even to the slightest olfactory stimulation and is still not overloaded by scent molecules and becomes inoperative for longer periods. The production of messengers can be stopped within milliseconds and therewith the basic condition of the cell can be recreated.

To make room for new olfactory information (and thereby eliminate any "olfactory background noise"), even the scent molecules themselves undergo a drastic change. Due to special enzymes, mainly contained in the supporting mucus, they are modified so strongly that they cannot re-bind to the receptor cells anymore – which they have to correspond to like lock and key. With the mucus, their fragments are washed out and swallowed through the nasopharynx later. New scent molecules can then arrive.

The mucus, produced by the supporting cells as well as the enzymes that are needed for the process of smelling, also contains specific antibodies that assure no germs wander into the brain. Due to the direct access that the olfactory nerve fibres, as primary sensory cells, have to the olfactory bulb in the brain, this could otherwise easily happen.

The intense contact between scent and olfactory cilia is the basis for olfactory perception. But how does the dog manage to distinguish the thousands of chemical substances that blow into its nose with every breath it takes, and how can it identify them as different scents?

Here again, the receptor proteins play an important role. Not only do scent components exist in a huge diversity, but there are also different receptor proteins. And this is what represents the great selectivity of the olfactory sensors. Not all scent molecules that reach the olfactory epithelium activate the olfactory cells to the same extent. There are always cells that react more strongly to a special scent than to others. Nevertheless, a dog's single olfactory receptor cell (like a human's) doesn't only react to a single very specific scent, but also intensively reacts to several other scent molecules built similarly chemically. Thus the olfactory sensory cells – similar to the gustatory cells – have a reaction spectrum that is rather broad and a little overlapping.

The nose needs variety

Olfactory receptor cells adapt very easily. That means when similar scent molecules, in similar quantities, regularly reach the olfactory cilia, the sensors get used to this specific olfactory spectrum and start reacting less and less. Even the brain simply starts to blank out such uninteresting smells. Inhaling a different fragrance with a varied consistence of molecules and/or concentration often helps awaken the tired receptors.

When following a track, mainly by zigzagging, dogs scent do the same without us having to teach them to do so. Furthermore, they do not inhale the air with one long deep breath when sniffing, but in a jerky way (whilst the space between the sniffing episodes is always the same). This, too, helps to keep the sensitive sensors going. At the end of such a sniff, the breath is usually held for a little while.

It is likely that scented air can thus reach even the most faraway olfactory cells – the ones at the back of the nose, as well as the ones at the roof of the palate.

The free nerve endings in the mucous membrane of the nose, such as the trigeminal

Irritating background smells can disturb even the fine nose of a search and rescue dog and can significantly complicate a search.

Smells that we can't even perceive can contain the most interesting information for dogs, news that can make them happy, but also make them insecure or even frightened. How strong the resulting reactions are depends on the animal's past experience.

nerve, react to special fragrances, for example, smells that we perceive as sharp. When the irritating fragrance is especially strong, it results in sneezing and thus a defence reflex. In dogs, this effect can be observed when they are walking along a busy road or enter a room filled with perfume.

How can the dog distinguish smells?
Dogs can not only perceive a whole range of different smells, but also differentiate them and identify certain fragrances. But how does this work?

On the basis of tissue samples of the olfactory epithelium, it was determined, that the infinite different olfactory receptors are not deliberately scattered along the olfactory epithelium, but are rather arranged in a sort of pattern. Those receptor types that react to similar fragrances are grouped together.

The concluding result is amazing, when the olfactory cells, stimulated by the same fragrance, and their axons leading to the olfactory bulb, were compared, those axons don't end anywhere in the "main fragrance processing headquarters", but meet – often in hundreds – at clearly defined arrival points, the so-called glomeruli.

That means that, at those small anatomically functional units of the olfactory system, the brain has the chance to distinguish the fragrances registered by the olfactory sensory cells of the nose for the first time. It takes this opportunity to immediately provide several other regions of the brain with the gained details – for instance the limbic system, the diencephalon and the pituitary gland or the dog's hypophysis, respectively. The effect is that emotions, such as joy, fear, hunger or specific hunting instincts, are prompted. The brain compares the incoming olfactory picture with unconscious memories and thereby gains further insights into this specific smell and what to do about it next. Associations are made now, and even the animal's degree of alertness and motivation can be influenced that way. Besides such emotional and affective behaviours, it also has an effect on different metabolic processes in the dog's body, as some olfactory elements interfere and control, for instance, the hormonal balance through the hypophysis.

The dog still doesn't have a consciously perceived olfactory impression. This can only develop when the information from its nose reaches the cerebral cortex. Now, finally, it can perceive and evaluate the specific smell and react to it consciously.

All this happens in less than a blink of an eye. And it enables the dog to show off this admirable differentiation of smells, that happens fast as lightning. It only needs half a second for identification!

Is the olfactory performance the same in all dogs?

There are differences in the individual olfactory capability of dogs. But genetics are not always involved. Besides the dog's breed and its age, other factors can influence the perception or rather identification of a specific smell – not least its motivation.

Selecting a single olfactory component from a pot pourri of the most different scent molecules is one of the dog's specialities, even when it is less distinctive than all the others. And the dog can even associate different smells at the same time.

The genetic influence on olfactory accuracy

Not all dogs show the same brilliant faculty of smell. Very short-nosed breeds, for instance, are usually in a measurably inferior position, compared to their cousins with longer noses. This is because they don't have enough space for an expanded olfactory epithelium inside their snub noses, although even their olfactory mucous membrane is arranged with complexity and put into huge folds, to gain a larger surface. For comparison, the short-nosed English Bulldog's olfactory epithelium has a surface of about 40 square centimetres, the much smaller Dachshund, with its long nose, has about 75 square centimetres.

As the concentration of olfactory cells hasn't increased, dogs with a shorter muzzle have notably less olfactory cells and therefore also significantly less smell-sensitive olfactory cilia than the long-nosed ones. And also the mouth smelling organ occupies a lot less space in a short skull than in a longer one, which decreases its olfactory perception.

Due to disadvantageous anatomic circumstances in the skull, the so-called brachycephalic (short-muzzled) dog breeds, especially, have problems in breathing, because less olfactory stimuli eventually reach their olfactory sensors. As a consequence of a decreased provision of oxygen, these dogs usually get tired easily and have to take much more frequent brakes on their – not so productive – sniffing trail.

It's not only the shape of the skull and muzzle that determines the dimensions of the olfactory epithelium, but also the dog's body size. The Dachshund's olfactory epithelium reaches up to 75 square centimetres, as already mentioned; the Fox Terrier's reaches up to 84 square centimetres and the German Shepherd's reaches about 150 square centimetres. The larger the olfactory epithelium, the more space there is for sensory cells. However, this additional placement isn't proportional to the size. Big dogs, with their larger olfactory epithelium, have less olfactory sensory cells in relation to smaller dogs with a smaller olfactory epithelium. The Dachshund has around 125 million olfactory cells, the Fox Terrier has about 147 million and the German Shepherd has roughly 225 million. A higher number of olfactory cells increases the olfactory accuracy (in this case the increase isn't proportional either) but it is not solely responsible for the dog's confidence in tracking. This depends furthermore on breed specific qualities and behaviours, as well as on individual disposition and, of course, on the dog's motivation and training standard.

The number of genes that are responsible for the equipment of the olfactory cilia, with manifold receptors, is totally independent of the different sizes of olfactory epithelia in various dog breeds. All dogs have the same number: about 1000. That means that the genetic potential for a super sensitive nose is the same in all dogs. Whether it is actually used is determined by the breed.

Also, the more or less yellow colouring of the olfactory epithelium and equally the intensity of colour of the nose leather, don't have any effect on the performance of the olfactory sensory cells and the dog's faculty of smelling.

An important factor in the evaluation of the olfactory organ's performance (the olfactory accuracy) is the olfactory threshold. When comparing different values, attention should be paid to whether it involves the perception threshold or the identification threshold. The threshold value that enables the dog to really identify a certain scent as such (for instance butyric acid) – and therefore its identification threshold – is usually much higher than the threshold value that enables it to perceive the scent, but not to attach a qualitative value to it. Certain substances cannot be distinguished from each other by considering the concentration of their threshold values, such as the fatty acids, butyric acid and propionic acid. Normally, olfactory threshold values consider the perception threshold.

Even the noses of dog breeds that have a smaller sized olfactory epithelium, and therefore a smaller number of olfactory cells, due to their skull anatomy, are way ahead of human noses with their 5-10 square centimetres of surface. By the way, the thickness of our olfactory mucous membrane of 0.006 millimetres is essentially inferior to the dog's of 0.12 millimetres.

For our dog's nose, there is no mystery about where we have been and with whom we have been in contact.

Improving the faculty of smelling

The humidity inside the dog's nose is crucial for a reliable scent identification. The dryer the olfactory mucous membrane, the lower the number of dissolved scent molecules in it and therefore the worse the olfactory perception. When the nose's performance ought to be continuously good, the working dog needs a lot of drinking water and, if necessary, its food should additionally be soaked in water.

Also, regular breaks should definitely be provided: only then will the animal's body and especially its mind be fresh and ready to go. It is this concentration particularly that contributes to good sensorial performances. It is not for nothing that motivation is the magic word when working together with the dog – for the dog, it is acknowledgement and stimulation at the same time.

By the way, motivation is not only restricted to treats, praise and playing with a ball. Interesting smells sprayed onto a piece of cloth and waved invitingly in front of its nose often work, too. As already mentioned, special olfactory information also increases the attention and strengthens the memory – not only in dogs. This is why resourceful company bosses scent the air in their open-plan offices, for instance, with citronella aroma: it distinctly increases the performance of the workers.

You shouldn't, however, use too large quantities of scent. They are annoying, counterproductive and they can even be harmful to your health – and this also applies to the dog.

Chemicals, such as those in tobacco smoke or car exhaust fumes, strain its sensitive olfactory epithelium and can therefore visibly reduce the olfactory perception. This aspect should be considered when search and rescue dogs have to work in the ruins, in clouds of exhaust fumes from the recovery vehicles. Although their olfactory performance is usually better than that of untrained dogs, such damaging background scents considerably affect their identification capability. The identification of human smells doesn't become easier that way – even if they have learned to focus only on this scent and broadly block out all the other olfactory stimuli.

By the way, it is not only the attention that ceases during longer missions, even modified breathing contributes to the reduction of the scent hound's olfactory performance. Tracking is hard work. Inexperienced dogs, especially, often start to pant quickly. In this way, they are not only breathing through the nose, but also through the mouth – past the olfactory sensory receptors. That means less transient scent molecules, reduced olfactory perception, and poorer scent discrimination.

Though olfactory learning and memory processes mainly happen in the dog's upper

The Bloodhound is unbeatable when it comes to following a trace of scent close to the ground. With its dizzily high number of olfactory sensory cells (more than 500 million), it has the most perfect nose amongst dogs. It can easily follow an eight-day old human track on asphalt and eventually identify the particular quarry. Also the skin folds in its face, the folded lop ears (that fan the smells to the nose) and the constant slobbering, contribute to this fantastic olfactory capability.

Two more good noses: The Labrador Retriever has 280 million olfactory sensory cells, the Beagle, 300 million on its olfactory epithelium.

brain centres, their origin is already at the lowest level of the olfactory system – the olfactory receptors.

The more frequently a dog perceives a certain smell or is offered this smell during training, specifically as a scent hound, the quicker and more effective the assimilation of the stimuli, as well as the signal transfer. The more often a certain sensory channel is used, the more effective it gets. Practising obviously also trains the sensory receptors and the channels in the nose – thus subtler and subtler concentrations of a certain smell can be perceived and the nose's performance is improved.

Even the dog's olfactory bulb is able to learn. Known smells trigger a different EEG (electroencephalogram) pattern in its cells, than unknown ones. Furthermore, the synaptic transmission of those nerve cells that are always used in synchronisation, is facilitated by frequent olfactory practice. This phenomenon – one of the cornerstones of learning – happens, for instance, when the registration of a certain smell is always accompanied by the stimulation of other clearly defined nerve cells, such as when a reward is given to the dog. As a result and in particular, those stimuli that are exceptionally important for the dog are preferentially transferred. This sensitising effect is enhanced when the four-legged student is very attentive.

Incidentally, the performance of the dog's nose can be restricted by an undersupply of the micronutrient zinc. Zinc seems to beneficially affect the performance of the canine nose.

Olfactory accuracy depends on the age

The dog's olfactory accuracy changes according to its age. In puppies the differentiated olfactory perception through the nose starts gradually and doesn't reach adult level before about 16 weeks of age. Over the years, it loses a bit of precision.

Although dogs keep their olfactory capability much longer than good eyesight or hearing, even with this sense, we have ageing processes – and this takes place at the level of the olfactory mucous membrane. The number of olfactory cilia, as well as olfactory sensory cells, decreases when growing old. Furthermore, the performance of basal and supporting cells decreases, so that fewer olfactory cells can be reproduced and the cells that are left are badly provided for. Whether the vomeronasal olfactory cells lose performance due to their age, and to what extent, is not known.

In pubescent, uncastrated females, the olfactory keenness reaches a peak on average every six months, as the sensitivity of the sense of smell fluctuates, according to the cycle, always with one peak during the female's heat. The increased oestrogen level in the female's blood is responsible for that. Besides central effects, oestrogens, among others, have a direct influence on the consistency of the mucous membrane in the regio olfactoria this is what probably causes a sensitisation of the receptors. The sensitivity of the vomeronasal organ also seems to be increased during these weeks – no wonder, as it is important to find a suitable partner for reproduction right now.

An aggravating decrease of the olfactory capability, up to complete loss, can also take

Dogs have a much bigger olfactory bulb than humans. They also have much bigger brain sections to deal with olfactory information.

place due to heavy infectious diseases like distemper, for instance, or due to metabolism disorders such as Cushing's disease, an adrenal glands disease.

Living without any olfactory capability must be harder for a dog than losing its sight or hearing, as it can hardly be compensated for through the use of the other senses.

Never mind which sense you look at: the often cited 'party effect' is achieved by the dog only perceiving what is really important to him and what he is concentrating on – even when there is a lot going on around him.

Smells in the long-term memory

We all smell all the time and with every breath we take, whether we are awake or sleeping. And nothing brands itself on the long-term memory more than smells, even for people. It's the same with dogs – only that their scent memory outstrips ours by far. Dogs can probably distinguish over a million different scent pictures from each other, even of the lowest concentration. But what is even more impressive is that they can store them for years – often even lifelong – in their memory. And that's not the only thing: they don't forget their individual experiences linked to every single one of those smells. Now why is that?

Dogs live in a completely different world of sensory perception to humans. Smells are much more important for them than for us and they are often of vital importance. The sense of smell, for instance, helps in finding food, a sexual partner or in deciding whether someone is friend or foe. All this mainly depends on the knowledge about, and the quick and clear perception of, different smells.

Dogs can perceive butyric acid for instance, the main ingredient of sweat, vaginal secretion and other excretions of specific groups but also of prey, a million times better than we can. They can even perceive this fatty acid when there are only 10,000 molecules in one millilitre of air – for which we would need 10 million. We, too, exude butyric acid more or less plentifully. No wonder that dogs show a deep interest in our routes.

Fruit flavourings such as amyl acetate (an important ingredient in bananas) are not so interesting for dogs as their sense of smell is not very sensitive to it. But if dogs are given banana regularly as a treat, they can gradually identify amyl acetate faster and faster. From then on they trace it enthusiastically wherever they can as it has now dramatically gained in importance for them. While dogs cannot perceive the scent of special fruits very well (even less well than we do), they stand head and shoulders above us when it comes to special flower smells. Why are they interested in flowers? That's a matter of guesswork.

Even dogs themselves are real scent manufacturers: their skin, with its countless different scent glands, is an excellent communication organ – with the mouth smelling organ as main sensor. Especially strong smelling are their paws and the anogenital region.

During the first months, the course of the olfactory memory is set – that's why an early exposure to a preferably wide range of smells (besides sounds and visual impressions) should be part of the accustomisation of the puppy to its environment.

The excretion of those glands, on the one hand, is controlled through the nervous system and, on the other, depends on the animal's hormonal status. The activity of the violet gland (also called precaudal gland) at the upside of the tail, close to the croup, is controlled by sexual hormones – this often shows in a circular hair loss in this region, especially in very active stud dogs (and sometimes even in "normal" male dogs).

Just follow your nose

One aspect of a dog's behaviour that looks almost like a miracle to us is this freezing in one place, followed by heavy sniffing. The dog will then suddenly break off in a certain direction and follow a track – a track that we can't even imagine, let alone guess whether it leads to the source or away from it. Dogs accomplish this incredible task because they are not only able to distinguish the different

It's probably their phenomenal olfactory memory that provides dogs with their fabulous and legendary orientation capability.

smells from each other within seconds, but also because in addition, they have the imperceptible ability to unmask even the smallest differences in concentration of one and the same olfactory picture.

They only need a few claw or footprints in a row, therefore, or about 3-5 seconds.

This exact capability of discrimination is probably achieved because the olfactory signals along the dog's particularly complex olfactory tract arrangement, stand out essentially sharper from each other than they do, for instance, in the case of humans. This is probably done through some kind of additional contrastive process, but how it really works is unknown.

What is it that determines such tiny olfactory differences in the feature of a track that the dogs react to so clearly? A variety of factors contribute to this – and almost always there are also micro organisms, such as bacteria, involved.

When a wild animal brushes along the edge of the forest, it leaves behind a trace of scrunched grass, squashed microbes and dirtied ground, at the same time glandular secretion from its paws or claws transfer to the ground. All together, this results in a typical footprint of the animal.

It also rubs special scent glands against branches or marks tree trunks, stones, grass and low bushes with faeces and urine. Furthermore, it loses lots of skin cells and little hairs, as well fluids smelling characteristically of its body surface that scatter in the air and gradually sink to the ground: This is further important information that determines its specific olfactory picture.

Nevertheless the dog still doesn't know in which direction the sender of all this data has moved.

Now the numberless microbes come into play – those that are on branches, on the grass, the ground and, for instance, on the dander and the hair of the wild animal. Depending on the species, these organisms subsist on the leaked plant saps, the microbes catapulted to the surface, or the animal's glandular secretion and body fluids. As soon as they go for these, in order to digest them, they not only modify their chemical structure but also their original smell. The more time the bacteria have, therefore, the more they transform; the more they transform, the stronger the olfactory modification of the olfactory picture on the track becomes. It is those perfectly unimaginable, tiny olfactory differences from one footstep to the next, from one dander to the next, that are enough for the dog to orientate itself.

If the track proceeded continuously, or if the bacteria didn't have enough time to modify the existing olfactory picture, the dog wouldn't get enough indications on where it is more recent and where it is older. Therefore, he wouldn't be able to identify the direction of the track.

Recognizing individual smells

Even when we are riding a bike and leave behind a seemingly continuous track (which will lack the typical foot-sweat), our dog can follow us without difficulties – when we have only left a few minutes before. With those millions of cells full of bacteria that we lose continually, and the glandular secretion released into the air from our body surface, we trail a characteristic fragrance that must seem like a beacon to our dog. This isn't surprising as we shuffle 10,000 odoriferous skin cells from each finger every hour throughout the day and from our entire body about 40 million. The butyric, uric and acetic acids contained therein are the ones that lead the dog, as he is simply a master at recognising those special fatty acids. As already mentioned, he can perceive butyric acid a million times better than we can, uric acid two million times better and acetic acid an amazing 100 million times!

Of course, our dog will also detect us at the end of this progressive journey and not the strange cyclist that started simultaneously, but chose a different route after a few metres. Our fragrance is absolutely individual; no other person in the world has the same – unless we have an identical twin with exactly the same genome. For body fragrances are genetically pre-programmed. They can only be slightly modified by nutritional habits. If our identical twin lived in a fundamentally different style, the dog could even identify this tiny olfactory difference, and tell us apart.

Despite the enthusiasm for the performance of the dog's cold nose, a little training is still necessary until the dog has learned to really follow a human track regularly.

Early practice, ideally during puppy hood, and with their closest human carer will be fun for the dog. It encourages its interest in various smells and in the search work itself – and it trains its complete olfactory system. It will need a lot more careful and directed training before it is finally able to follow a strange person, whose individual olfactory picture it has only inhaled from a so-called olfactory example (for instance a slipper), several kilometres.

Many dogs prefer to use their excellent noses for trailing – thanks to their wonderful net of tiny blood vessels (see box on page 59), they can hang on for the chase longer than most of their victims, even in intense heat. The Flat Coated Retriever in the picture has had an easy task, retrieving a shot rabbit.

The dog's sense of smell perceives many things: the sparse olfactory traces of a drowning victim that rise to the water surface inside air bubbles; the jets of air that get through to the surface, via subtle cracks, shortly before an earthquake; or the modified smells of the skin and the urine of a cancer-sufferer. These are just a few examples.

Alteration of the track odour

A track cannot always be worked out everywhere at the same level and a certain olfactory pattern cannot always be located in the distance equally fast: Heat, extreme wetness or dryness, and also heavy winds aggravate the search.

A concrete floor is the most difficult terrain for following a purely ground-based track as the scent molecules vanish especially quickly here. When the ground is warmer than the air, the scent molecules soar into the air; when the ground is colder, they prefer to stay on the ground. On humid (not extremely wet!), soft earth smells can diffuse better than when the ground is dry.

Smells up in the air drift apart through the wind and are easily diluted. When it is dry they sink to the ground more slowly than in humid weather.

Varying search behaviour

Besides the modification of the smell through bacterial metabolic processes, the age of a scent trail also influences the actual search behaviour of the dog. When the track is recent and glandular secretions and cells are mainly still hovering in the air, the dog usually keeps its nose up in the air and searches more broadly and often even beside the actual footsteps. When the track is a little older and most of the scent molecules have already sunk to the ground, the dog directs itself more towards the ground.

Of course, the scent trail shouldn't be too old, otherwise the typical scents have almost vanished completely, and the dog has no chance to perceive them any more, let alone follow them successfully – unless he belongs to that brilliant breed of Bloodhounds.

According to the circumstances, the dog will always point its sensitive olfactory organ to where the concentration of the scent it is seeking is highest in order to find the smell and follow the track. The fact that specific breeds nevertheless tend to pick up the scent on the ground or in the air is down to their different – and breeder selected – genetic disposition. Many of the hunting dog breeds are grouped among the typical ground searchers, in contrast to herding dog breeds that enjoy having their noses high up in the air.

But dogs can learn to adapt their search behaviour to our preferences. So-called tracking dogs orientate mainly by footprints, disturbed vegetation and ground. They keep their nose close to the ground and are not interested in associated olfactory information in the air. Scent hounds, however, work mainly with their nose above the ground, and try to find the scent originating, for instance, from hair and cells sinking to the ground, in that way. Some search and rescue dogs pick up the scent even higher in the air – they lift their noses up high into the air to locate the sought fragrance. They usually work completely detached from any footprints or a person's specific olfactory pattern – in contrast to man-trailing dogs that specialise in staying solely on the track of one special person, regardless of whether they find it on the ground, the wall of a house, or in the air.

"Stereo smelling"

The dog has two nose openings that are separated from each other by the nasal septum and that have two parallel airstreams passing through. This is an ideal prerequisite for a sort of stereo smelling, but most dogs' nostrils lie quite close together so a special resolution doesn't seem to be likely. Looking further back up the nostrils where they are widely stilted to both sides of the nose leather, it becomes more likely.

Indeed, dogs are said to be able to distinguish between the two airstreams in their nose and in that way collect important information on the olfactory intensity gradient. Of course, they could also just turn the head to the source of smell and make sure that they get enough information on the origin of the smell.

But with the nose close to the ground, it is definitely an advantage to be able to

Orientation by means of scent allows a look into the past. Smells bypass hindrances and even spread out unopposedly in the dark. Pinpointing a smell accurately in the distance, however, is more difficult than pinpointing the position of optical or acoustical signals.

distinguish signals differing minimally from each other, without having to move the head. Especially as the necessary central connections also exist: The part of the olfactory epithelium located on the left side of the body sends its nerve fibres to the left part of the olfactory bulb; the one located on the right side sends them to the right part. Furthermore the recognition time of smells perceived simultaneously through both nostrils is measurably shorter than the recognition time of individually perceived smells. (At least this was proven to be the case in humans – a smell that reaches us at the same time through both nostrils has a stronger effect.)

The dog's nose – a brain cooler

At the base of the heart, the arteries that supply the brain branch out into a net of hundreds of small, extremely thin-walled blood vessels. This so-called rete mirabile (wonderful net) is covered by a dense network of veins that obtains its blood from the dog's nose and mouth area. The venous blood is colder than the arterial blood, therefore it absorbs much warmth from the arterial blood and with this protects the heat-sensitive brain from overheating. Furthermore, as the blood circulation in both vessel networks works counter clockwise, the cooling is especially effective. Panting is even more effective: as the breathing rate increases, the evaporation rate of water on the mucous membrane in the oral and nasal cavity increases at the same time. As a result, the mucous membrane and the blood in the vessels cool down simultaneously.

Due to the small thermoregulatory surface, the cooling effect of the rete mirabile is clearly inferior in short-nosed breeds. Therefore those breeds are much more heat-sensitive than the long-nosed ones.

Dogs cannot only smell many more things than we can, but what they smell is also much better differentiated and evaluated. Furthermore they usually attach more importance to smells.

Dogs see
differently

Warmth, coldness, touch, pain: a puppy a few weeks old can register all these stimuli very well – and can react to them appropriately. Even a small nose is already sniffing around enthusiastically. The mouth olfactory organ perceives the most interesting species-specific smells; the olfactory epithelium, located in the nasal cavity, is very eager to perceive the various new smells all around. Nevertheless, all this happens in complete darkness and silence. Then suddenly – around the 13th day of its life – slight beams of light reach the eye's retina and give the young puppy a totally new sensory impression: light. This is the moment when its eyelids start to open up more and more. But as mentioned, the eye organ is not in complete working order yet, the sight impressions remain vague and blurry for the present moment. Normally, it takes at least two weeks for the puppy to perceive its environment sharply and correctly – the retina of the dog's eye is fully developed after about two months.

It is moving, high-contrast objects that the small four-legged animal can perceive best. During these first days of its life, he almost does not perceive non-moving objects or colours, because the photosensitive pigments of his eyes need time to develop. The same applies to the pigments that determine the colour of its eyes. The puppy only has few of those pigments in the first weeks of its life. That's why its eyes seem to be blue. Little-by-little, the proportion of those pigments that count among the melanins in the iris grow and thus the colouring of its eyes gets darker: The more melanin molecules exist, the more brown the iris. Dog eyes with a rather greenish-yellow or yellow-brown colour are attributed to too many fat cells in the iris. Cells containing fat change the iris to a more yellow colour.

The genetic information determines which colour shade the eyes will ultimately have and how uniformly the coloured spots are distributed in the iris tissue. This is what's important: the more pigments the eye has, the less sensitive it reacts to bright light, as the iris functions as a sun protection filter for the light receptors in the eye. Light blue eyes, where only the back region of the iris is slightly pigmented, and eyes with a high proportion of the colour white, so-called glass eyes, are especially at risk.

During the time in the uterus, the puppy's eyelids barely touch each other. Later on, around the 40th day of pregnancy, the eyelids grow together, presumably for the protection of the eyeball.

The eyelids begin to open, starting close to the nose, after about two weeks. The puppy only has a diffused bright-dark perception at that time.

The typical blue of a puppy's eyes is created by a purely physical phenomenon, the refraction of light. Melanin globules, bringing colour, are stored in the iris gradually.

As the dog's eye lens is bent, it means they have better visual accuracy over medium than long distances. However, they can't project images sharply that are less than 50 cm away because the lens has little elasticity.

The passage of light through the dog's eye

The light reaches the anterior chamber through the transparent anterior front of the eye, the cornea. There it hits the iris, which regulates the amount of light that enters the eyeball. It lets the light pass through a round opening in the middle, the pupil.

The width of this opening, that is the size of the pupil, is controlled by a reflex: with only little environmental brightness, the opening is large (the pupil is adjusted in width) in order to catch as many rays of light as possible. With very bright light, it is adjusted to a small size, to reduce the amount to protect the sensitive photoreceptors. In relation to the size of their eyes, dogs can open their pupils extremely wide - much wider than we can. This is already a first hint of their ability to see better in twilight.

Emotional influences and mental stress can also change the size of the pupils. When afraid, but also with happiness and contentment, the pupil gets especially big. The same applies to the dog being mentally challenged. The greater the attention, the larger are its pupils. When the dog gets tired, the size of its pupils constantly changes. When the dog is in a rather aggressive mood or in pain, the pupils are dilated.

Via the pupil, the light reaches a bent lens which bundles the light and projects it on the retina at the eyeground via the vitreous body. The sharpness of the object's picture also depends on the degree of curvature of this lens. The thicker the lens, the more refractively it functions: the eye is regulated to seeing things that are close by. As the lens is flexibly located in the eye, via fibres and tiny muscles, its curvature can be controlled by a reflex. If it becomes flat, the refraction decreases so that more distant objects can be seen sharply. This automatic regulation process is called accommodation. The more elastic a lens is, the better it can accommodate, especially to objects nearby.

As the dog's eye lens is pretty bent, when it comes to adapting to distances, dogs can see sharply over medium rather than long distances. And as the lens loses its elasticicty, even in the early years of life, it becomes less adaptable. The area within which the dogs can focus, which means they can project a sharp image of the environment on their retina, therefore is not very large. In fact, it's much smaller than for human beings. But for them, it is less important if the image they see is very sharp anyway, because dogs pay attention to optic contrasts and movements. Additionally, they count on their ability to see even when there's barely light. Due to the extreme wideness of the pupil, this leads to strong stray light effects and therefore to a faded, rather fuzzy image. So why should they put additional effort into the fine focusing for all distances? After all, they have a fantastic nose for everything nearby!

Nevertheless, in the course of evolution, a possibility of compensation was developed

All surfaces have to be as smooth and clear as possible in a well functioning optic organ. When the production of tears decreases as the dog gets older, the cornea of the eye gets dry and its visual accuracy decreases. The ability to see decreases also when, over the years, the lens turns blurry because of crystalline sediments.

even for this handicap. Dogs' eyes have big lenses that can bundle stray light a bit better than smaller ones would – thus the caught image gets a bit brighter.

The retina

In order to be able to visually perceive the environment, the electromagnetic waves that are respectively sent or reflected by certain objects, have to target special receptors that react to those incentives – which means light-sensitive sensory cells, the so-called photoreceptors. There are two types of these sensors in the retina of the dog's eye: the stretched rods and the clubbed cones. As secondary sensory cells without their own nerve fibres leading to the brain, they only function as incentive receiving structures. That means they catch streams of light and turn them into electric impulses. The light-sensitive pigment molecules, the photo pigments, that are located in the cell membrane are responsible for this process. These pigments are able to absorb light with a certain wavelength. Within only a few picoseconds (billionth of a second), they then experience a chemical change, that finally leads to the receptor cell developing an electric signal. As long as it crosses a certain threshold, it is sent to the neighbouring nerve cells located in the retina of the eye, to so-called ganglia among others. This happens via synaptic contacts. It then reaches higher parts of the brain, where it is evaluated and experienced with awareness.

Rods contain a much higher proportion of pigments than cones do. For this reason, they are much more sensitive to light than cones and enable the dog to see even with little light, for example at dawn. (A single rod can be stimulated even by a single light quantum, the smallest amount of light there is.) As a larger number of rods reach one ganglion, the effect is even bigger. Much more light is caught, admittedly at the expense of visual accuracy, as the exact three-dimensional allocation of light information is therefore decreased.

It's a totally different story with the cones: because of their smaller proportion of pigments, they admittedly are less sensitive to light and allow the dog to see only when it is brighter. As a cone always sends its light information only to one ganglion cell, a much higher visual accuracy is the result. In order not to let this advantage be reduced by additionally produced rod signals, the transmission of the rod signals is blocked whenever there is enough light for the cone pigments to come into action. Thus the rods are responsible for the dog's so-called scotopic vision, as the cones are for the photopic vision.

In the human retina, the 100-125 million rods are already in the majority, compared to the 3-6 million cones. With the dog, that can see much better at dawn, one can find an even greater decrease in cones, in favour of the highly sensitive rods.

The optic resolution and thus the vision detail, does not only depend on the lightness and the central connection of the sensory cells but also on their density. The more light receptors are available, the better is the sight, i.e. the more single, neighbouring image points the eyes still perceive as single light impulses. In fact, there is a special area (called macula) in the dog's retina, where the density of the photoreceptors is extraordinarily high.

This area of the retina is somehow comparable to our so-called spot of the sharpest

In breeds that mainly orientate optically, the macula is said to be especially big and rich in cones. Generally the cones in the centre of the retina represent about 20 per cent of all receptors.

vision (= yellow spot, fovea centralis), located directly opposite the pupil, but it is less closed off from the neighbouring tissue. It's remarkable that this area of the retina is not small and round like ours, but stretches over a rather long, vertical oval area of the eyeground: an ideal adjustment mechanism to the dog's habitat and behaviour. He is able to sharply perceive optic stimuli that reach this strip of the retina especially well – for example, a prey that darts across the horizon.

Similar to the increased central representation of the tactile receptors of the face and paw area, this sense area in the dog's brain is also over proportionately big in its so-called visual cortex. This also adds to the enormous importance of the macula when it comes to the optic orientation of the dog.

The weird glow of a dog's eyes in a spotlight is caused by the light-reflecting cell layer behind the retina that dramatically increases the amount of light used.

The tapetum lucidum – a low light amplifier

The various anatomic and physiological adjustments within the eye that try to catch even the slightest ray of light show how important it is for dogs to find their way via optic impressions of their environment. This includes an efficient reflecting surface at the back of their retina, the tapetum lucidum. Consisting of 10 to 20 staggered, tile-like layers of cells, this half-round reflecting layer covers the complete upper area of the eyeground. It increases the eye's use of light by reflecting the rays at twilight so that once again they reach the light-sensitive sensory cells on the retina. As these cells are located on the back of the retina anyway, which means at the side, turned away from the vitreous body, this is easily possible. Interestingly enough, the retina doesn't have any light receptors on its front, but only on its back layers.

Every single tapetum cell has innumerable latticed rod-shaped structures that contain large amounts of zinc and riboflavin (vitamin B2). Zinc, especially, is highly reflective. It's the zinc that mainly reflects the incoming light – namely the light that isn't already absorbed by the photo pigments when entering the pupil, or isn't swallowed by other pigment cells in the retina.

The dog's tapetum lucidum is so efficient that it should increase the dog's optic ability to see in twilight by an astonishing 50 per cent. But the perceived image gets a bit blurred and fuzzy through the higher diffusion of the light. Whether the improved light use at night is really enough to also activate the cones in the retina, as is sometimes claimed, remains a matter for discussion. If the achieved light intensity was enough, dogs should even be able to perceive different colours in twilight, as the cones aren't only responsible for the ability to see at daylight but also to see colours.

As the crystalline structures within the tapetum lucidum refract light that much, a variety of colours ranking from blue-green to green, yellow or orange, that is reflected when bright light reaches the dog's eye at night (= prism effect), is produced. The exact colour in which the eyes fluoresce in each individual case also depends on the angle of incidence of the light, as the reflecting layer doesn't have the same thickness everywhere. In its central regions, it consists of many more cell layers than at its edges.

Additionally, the pigments that are located in the tapetum lucidum, and also the ones that give the colour to the connective tissue

This eye is only poorly pigmented, causing the light blue of the iris. It also probably lacks the tapetum lucidum, as its reflections usually prevent the visibility of the red blood vessels of the retina and the eyeground.

of the retina, contribute to the individual appearance of our four-legged companion's eye glow at night – where even each of its eyes can have a different colour.

If you now go outside at night, armed with a torch, to test which colour expression your dog's eyes have, and then find that you cannot see any reflection (or only in one of its eyes), then it might be the case that your dog carries the merle factor. Besides the desired brindling or the irregular mottling of their hair, heterozygote animals usually also show changes in the pigment balance of their sense system (for example a deficit of iris or retina pigments) and/or a complete or partial lack of the tapetum lucidum and its special pigments. Certainly this is a disadvantage for these animals and their optic ability to orientate, nevertheless, one can also find good herders and police dogs among the merle carriers with such deficits.

The identification of light and dark parts of the visual field – the contrast perception – requires shape vision. With dogs, the perception zone of light, meaning the visible spectrum, probably ranges from approximately 400 to roughly 700 nanometres.

Image recognition via contrasts

The so-called achromatic colours, meaning black, white and the grey tones, are only characterised by their different brightness. One single light sensitive colouring that absorbs the respective rays of light, is enough to perceive them, so that they can then be transmitted to the brain through the optic tract as electric signals. The comparison of different wavelengths, as with the colour vision, is not necessary here. Instead, in this case, the activity and the connection of the nerve cells, which are switched behind the light receptors, are important. It's from them that the visual cortex retrieves its achromatic detailed information, that tells whether a certain object is lighter or darker than the environment, and how clearly the registered difference in brightness is recognised.

Dogs are able to recognise minimal differences in brightness and to experience their world (apart from its coloured parts) in very delicate shades of grey. With little brightness, the rods fulfil the task of contrast perception; with lots of light, the cones take over this job. As the focus of the dog's visual system is the border area between the different levels of brightness, meaning the contours of an object, the shape vision, especially, is sharpened. The dog's shape perception is so good that he can, for example, clearly distinguish a circle from an ellipse. In the same way, he can recognise rectangles or octagons. The human's ability to distinguish different levels of brightness is also excellent, but the darker the environmental light is, the better our four-legged companions do when it comes to recognising tiny light–dark differences.

The latest analysis gave rise to the question, whether there are breed-related differences when it comes to a dog's ability to differentiate different levels of brightness. It requires extensive surveys to finally clarify this question.

Also, the other (chromatic) colours like blue, green, yellow and red can be described due to their different brightness. However, not exclusively, as their shade (depending on the wavelength of the light), as well as their colour saturation (depending on the proportion of uncoloured incentives), both contribute to the general impression. In order to not only recognise the brightness of an object but also its colouring, it requires various different vision pigments, which each sensitively react to different spectrum areas of the light. And they can also be found in the dog's retina.

How dogs perceive colours

The rods always come in one single variant. All contain the same pigment, rhodopsin, which is also called visual purple. With these rods, a differentiation between different wavelengths is not possible. The light perception via rods is therefore colourless. As rhodopsin reacts with particular sensitivity in the blue-green spectrum area during dawn, a dog probably perceives blue objects brighter than objects of another colour, but still not colourful.

It's a different case with the cones. They exist in different variants. There are two of them in the dog's retina. The difference lies in the pigments that are staggered in the cell membranes and in the fact that each absorbs different bandwidths of the visible light. The maximum spectral sensitivity of the one cone type – the maximum absorption of its special pigment – is a wavelength of about 430 nanometres, which means in the short-wave area. The other is a wavelength of about 570 nanometres, therefore in the long-wave area. The cone type especially sensitive in the short-wave area (the blue cones) is called blue receptor; the cone type especially sensitive in the long-wave area (the red cones) is called red receptor.

As each of those wavelengths stimulates the two types of cone in a very special proportion, according to the absorption ability of their photo pigments, the brain can differentiate the wavelength according to the comparison of this information. Dogs can therefore differentiate colours of different shades and saturation.

Their colour-sensitivity is in fact pretty high, except with a wavelength in the area of 480 nanometres (that is blue-green), where it's almost zero. Dogs therefore don't perceive blue-green as a colour; they always perceive it as white or grey, respectively. That is because, at this wavelength, which is also called the neutral point, both types of cone of the retina are equally stimulated, and thus a comparison of the signals is not possible. Therefore dogs are dichromats, meaning animals whose retina only has two types of cone instead of three, like human beings – typical trichromats. Dogs are lacking a type of cone with a special pigment for the medium-wave, the green area of the light spectrum, therefore a green cone or green receptor. The colour they lack, therefore, is green.

The lack of a receptor for the perception of the colour green defines the clinical picture of deuteranopia with human beings. Therefore, it's assumed that dogs perceive colours similarly to human beings that suffer from a fault in their retina, also called blindness to green (not blue cone monochromacy!). In the area of violet, indigo and blue shades, those people have the ability to see colours almost similarly to healthy people. Due to the lack of the green receptor, they cannot however perceive colours in the wavelength of 480 nanometres at all or at least only with changes and, furthermore, they confuse certain shades of colours.

It's the same with dogs. In wavelength areas between 420 and roughly 480 nanometres, meaning the colour impressions violet, indigo or blue, their colour perception is so perfectly developed that they can identify those colours, and also perfectly differentiate

Corresponding to their adjustment to little light intensity, dogs pay much more attention to light-dark perception than to the recognition of colours.

Visible colour spectrum showing nanometres: canine above, human below.

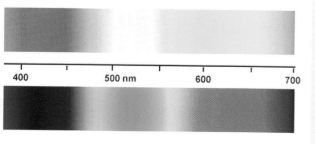

KH Widmann 2004

them from each other. This even applies in cases where the shade of the colour only varies by wavelengths of 2 nanometres.

If one wants to train a dog via colour incentives or simply entertain the dog, one should therefore work with motivation objects of the colour blue, indigo or violet. Here, one can assume that the dog really recognises the colour and does not only react to the brightness of the objects.

With higher wavelengths of the visible spectrum, the dog's ability to see decreases, and its colour sensitivity declines. Certain shades of turquoise, for example, aren't perceived as a colour by the dog, he rather perceives them as grey or white. The more the wavelengths approach the red area in the spectrum, the more the dog perceives them as yellow. He perceives red as bright yellow.

Due to the lack of additional cone pigments in the medium-wave area, dogs have less ability for the fine comparison of colours. Therefore, within this spectrum area, they confuse certain colours, like green with yellow, green with red or yellow with red. The colours that we perceive as red, yellow, orange, brown or yellow-green or green respectively, which we can still easily categorise into different shades, cannot be differentiated by dogs. But they can absolutely differentiate those colours from achromatic light, for instance white. The same applies to blue-violet shades. Although dogs cannot perceive, for example, green as we can, to them green still looks completely different from violet or blue.

This can also be a means of differentiation and can improve the orientation.

The dog's spectral sensitivity for blue shades is the greatest. The red ball appears as yellow to him and can almost not be distinguished from the green grass. But of course the four-legged animal can see the ball – not least because of its fast movement.

This means, our dogs' world isn't colourless as we used to think; it is simply limited to a smaller colour spectrum than ours, namely to blue-violet shades, white and yellow shades. Admittedly, the colours appear a bit paler to dogs. That is because dogs have fewer cones in their retina. An orange-red toy in the green grass is much harder for the dog to recognise, as the two colours appear far too similar to the dog. However, he will quickly find the toy with the help of other senses. But if the dog is supposed to find a retrieving buck for field work, and should clearly differentiate between grass or soil colours respectively, blue or white coloured objects are much more appropriate. Dogs can anyway recognise shades of blue much better, due to their high colour sensitiveness in this wavelength area. And most of the colours can easily be distinguished from white.

The orange-green and pure orange coloured dummies, often used in retrieving, contribute more to the human being's visual orientation than to that of the dog. A retrieving buck that is wrapped into a white sock and placed vertically on the grass, can be recognised by the dog much faster – with the help of its colour sense as well as the increased contrasts.

Should a dog's ability to smell be trained and should the optic orientation be avoided, one can make use of this deficit in the ability to distinguish colours, for example by using a retrieving buck that can hardly be recognised by the dog. A green dummy on a rich green coloured meadow would suffice.

Whenever the orientation should be made easy for the dog (as with agility), one should think about whether the dog can really distinguish between the used colours. If you already have course elements that appear colourless to the dog (for example elements that have orange coloured stripes), you need not throw them into the dustbin, as colours simply aren't as important to the dog as they are to us. They can easily find their way even without coloured marks.

Movement perception

In terms of optic orientation, it is much more important for dogs to scan their field of vision for moving objects as thoroughly as possible and to clearly categorise them as quickly as possible, as their survival may depend on this. Also, human eyes are adjusted to recognise movements. With dogs, however, even the slightest twitch, that we can no longer recognise, triggers closer examination. Put into figures: they recognise movements at least 10 times better than we do.

This is due to their ability to distinguish single light-dark incidents, even if they appear quickly after one another. And this in turn is due to the numerous nerve cells in their visual cortex, sensitive to movements and directions, which show a very small reaction time and a conspicuously high rate of signal transmission.

Dogs are real flicker-filmmakers. The temporary border frequency of their vision, the so-called flicker fusion rate, is astonishingly high. Admittedly, it's not as high as that of a fly, but they still by far outstrip us mainly visual oriented humans. Dogs still recognise 80 flashes of light per second as a single event (we can recognise 60 at the most); with higher frequencies they fuse into a constant light. It also depends at which point exactly the amount of rays of light that reaches the retina arrive. The higher the amount of light, the higher the critical flicker rate. Therefore, it's no surprise, dogs recognise movements, especially at twilight, so much better than we do.

It's also their greater temporary resolution that enables dogs to enjoy unspoilt televi-

Thanks to the strong movement detectors in the dog's brain, he recognises even the slightest twitch. The light sensitive receptors in its retina and the low-light amplifier in its eyeground make such a fine movement perception possible, even in the slightest half-light, and out of the corner of its eye.

sion viewing comparable with the modern devices of the 100-Hz generation. The older devices appear to them rather as a mid-ranged slide show than moving pictures. However, for the dog, watching television is understandably not half as spectacular as chasing a 'rabbit' in the form of a bouncing ball. Therefore we should invest our money into an appropriate toy for our companion rather than into a new TV, and should spend moved our time with our dog!

As the visual impulse change is very important for dogs, their eyes are constantly searching for it. They are permanently scanning their field of vision through tiny movements of their eyeballs.

Therefore, even stationary objects project moving pictures on their retina. The percep-

This 10-week old puppy is following the gestures of the human with great interest. Incidentally: considering the size of the dog's skull in comparison to that of the human proportionately, dogs have much larger eyes.

Eye contact is an essential element of communication between dog and man – but a constant demand for eye contact stresses the dog.

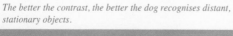

The better the contrast, the better the dog recognises distant, stationary objects.

Even dogs with visual difficulties rarely miss such a flying treat. If it falls on the grass, he will use his nose in order to look for it.

Finding lost sheep? That's no problem for this sheepdog!

The dog's sharp power of observation, mainly focussed on recognition of the slightest movements, also pays off when catching small prey.

tion of shape benefits especially from this. Nevertheless, it's much harder for dogs to perceive non-moving objects than for us. If we stand still in front of a tree, only 30 meters away from the dog, he can often not identify us visually. Sometimes, he even doesn't see us when we then perform a slow movement, because the dog misses this movement. However, he can easily perceive us waving quickly from a distance of 500 meters.

Both events admittedly astonish but no longer puzzle us. The same applies to the fact that we never remain completely hidden from the dog, even despite unperceived contours in front of the aforementioned tree. We reveal ourselves by our smell and with every rustle or crack that we cause, as nothing remains hidden to the dog's perfect sense of smell and its perfect sense of hearing.

A fine flair for every movement

It's really fascinating to observe how, for example, retrievers or herders can be guided via clear gestures and hand signals, even over distances of up to 1 kilometre. What's just as astonishing is the dogs' ability to understand and interpret even the slightest pointer, even minimal mimic changes. Maybe even when their eyes almost closed, they are observing us constantly, out of the corner of their eye. What other explanation could there be for their ability to register an exchange of looks, even when they are half-asleep. Hasn't that already happened to you as well? You are just considering whether to play together with your dog and you let your gaze wander to the ball on the mantelpiece (without even turning your head), and suddenly your playmate starts to stretch in order to be prepared.

The dog follows the movement of our eyeballs especially, and can even perfectly interpret our intentions with some practice. A change in the line of vision is enough to make a dog turn its attention in that direction. You don't believe it? Just have a try! Kneel down in front of your dog, having placed a toy or a treat to the left and the right of the room. Put your hand behind your back and, keeping your head as still as possible, look into your dog's eyes with a friendly expression. Now, quickly move your eyeballs, let's say to the left.

Repeat this a few times. It won't take long before your four-legged pupil has understood that he is supposed to run to that side.

The three-dimensional vision of dogs with long skulls is a little inferior to their relatives that have a rather roundly-shaped skull, other than that they are able to perceive hand signals out of the hindmost corner of their eyes.

Unconscious signs probably tell our dogs even more. Maybe it's exactly that uncharacteristic eyeball movement that gives epilepsy seruice dogs the crucial hint to the imminent spasm of their human charges. According to the changes that appear simultaneously in the facial expression, the gestures and the breathing rhythm of their patients that those so-called "seizure-alert dogs" surely also register, they know what is about to happen and can give a warning to their owner. Thanks to their incredible powers of observation, dogs can probably register the almost invisible twitching of the facial muscles and typical strain in the muscles of the upper part of the body of epilepsy patients about to go through a spasm.

Certainly their fine powers of observation aren't only helpful to dogs in their interactions with us but also with their equals. Their mimic signals admittedly are no longer as strongly developed as those of wolves, but, not least, dogs communicate with each other visually. The importance of communication via visual expressions can be demonstrated through the misunderstandings that arise when, for example, animals are wearing a fur curtain in front of their eyes, which hides any facial expression or when they have a breed-specific modified tail, that can be misleading for their opposite numbers.

Due to their anatomically different locations, the right and the left eye each perceive a slightly different area of the environment. via the projections on the two retinas these are slightly shifted towards each other. From this relative difference, the brain retrieves its information that finally leads to the perception of three-dimensionality.

A means of measuring the ability to see is by the number of nerve fibres that form the optic tract. Human vision nerves consist of roughly 1 million nerve fibres, the dog's olfactory nerve only 170,000. This nevertheless doesn't mean that dogs completely outstrip human beings optically. There is simply a different emphasis within their optic systems: a much higher sensitivity to light and movement at lower visual accuracy and colour perception.

Three-dimensional vision

Alongside good communication with other dogs and man, the ability to pinpoint any movement promises a good successful hunt – especially if it's possible to correctly estimate the distance to the prey. Optically, dogs can't do that very well (but they can rely on their smell and on their sense of hearing with confidence). This is due rather to their eyes being located at the side of their heads, which gives them a pretty good all-around view, but no precise ability to sense the position, location, orientation and movement of their body and its parts and therefore a bad estimation of distances.

Visual field versus field of vision

Each eye can perceive a certain area of the environment, the size of which corresponds to the so-called monocular (one-eyed) visual field. If one looks with both eyes, the binocular (two-eyed) visual field, that is, in comparison to the monocular visual field, the more laterally the eyes are sitting in the bony skull.

The larger its visual field, the further the dog can see to the back, even without moving the eyes. If it moves its eyes (sideways, it can move them to a maximum of 50 degrees; upward or downward, to a maximum of 40 degrees), its view is much larger. This enlarged visual field is called the field of vision. The dog can, of course, additionally move its head and/or body and can therefore respectively enlarge its field of vision, or its binocular visual field across the whole area.

Dogs generally have a much larger visual field than we do, with our eyes located head-on and a visual field of about 180 degrees. However, there are significant differences with certain breeds. Animals with long snouts achieve a binocular visual field of 270 degrees at the most. For animals with short snouts, that have eyes located more towards the nose, it's clearly smaller. With the Boston Terrier, for example, it extends to roughly 200 degrees. So, contrary to what one would expect, this doesn't only involve disadvantages for the short muzzled animals.

The visual field consists of three different parts that contribute in different ways to the overall visual impression. One region is located in the middle and can be seen by both eyes. This region is much larger for animals that have eyes lying closely together than for animals with eyes further apart. Then there are two side areas, each of which can only be seen by one eye. It's the region in the middle especially, from which an exact three-dimensional perception is possible. The two side areas only contribute a little to a good three-dimensional impression. The advantage of an enlarged region, therefore, is the good three-dimensional perception of the environment. The larger this region, the better the three-dimensional sense. Therefore, dogs with short snouts are one step ahead in terms of three-dimensional perception.

Of course, dogs with slender skulls can also see three-dimensionally and can correctly estimate distances, otherwise they would probably not be able to shepherd or to hunt prey.

They are simply not as good at it as others with more round heads and flatter faces.

The more frontal the eyes are positioned, the better pronounced the depth perception is. In dogs the angle of three-dimensional vision is between 60 and 90 degrees, depending on the animal's skull – in humans it's up to 120 degrees.

To provide their brain with additional information about distances, these animals move their heads much more often, when focussing for example, which makes a closer object move faster into their visual field than a more distant one. They also orientate themselves with the help of comparative scales of far distant objects and with contour overlapping, the light or shadow on distant objects (This applies to all dogs no matter their skull anatomy).

When the eyesight weakens

From the middle age on, a decline of the dog's visual system takes place, especially with the retina and its photoreceptors. Opacities, or a decreased tear fluid production, due to old age can weaken the vision as well. Normally, pathological processes are to blame when the eyesight is already significantly weakened at an earlier point and the dog finally goes completely blind, as with Progressive Retina Atrophy (PRA). This is a slowly progressing reduction of blood vessels in the retina (and therefore an undersupply of the photoreceptors). Or Retina-Dysplasia (RD), in which the retina – and also the sensory cells – increasingly become detached from the eyeground. Often such diseases are genetically determined, which is why strong breeding regulations are in place to attempt to prevent their spreading.

Defects in the dog's sense system can also be linked to less pigments in the coat, as with certain pure white breeds, amongst which some individuals are already born blind or deaf, respectively (see next chapter).

One often does not recognise a dog's blindness for a long time as he increasingly uses other senses, for example the sense of touch via the paws and vibrissae, to compensate for the loss. The body contact and the voice of the human being are, therefore, especially important for a dog whose eyesight is affected or who is blind. For example, when our 12-year-old Labrador bitch wants to go down a steep staircase, she sits down in front of it barking and waits until we come running and accompany her downstairs, while gently touching her at her flank or calmly talking to her. The way she barks in such situations is very typical and absolutely unmistakable for us – as she has never expressed this kind of bark before in her long life. An elderly dog will create a totally new sound only for the purpose of bringing something to the attention of its human.

Ears that "hear the grass grow"

The dogs are peacefully slumbering on their cushions – grandma Tessa on her stomach, her head between her front paws. Bonnie is closely snuggling up to her. Carol, the youngest one, is lying on her back, all four legs stretched into the air. The humans are sitting at the table, drinking coffee and chatting. What a perfect Sunday. Suddenly and as if prearranged, the dogs move convulsively with eyes wide open. Lively little Carol is already standing, ready for action. "Ready? Let's go." What had happened? What had woken the group up? Oh yes! Once more one of us had said, too early, the magic words: "Let's go for a walk!" Despite the fact we had agreed to use one of our numerous fantasy words for this special event, until the time was right....

One more new experience for the puppies. At first, sounds are dull; but they get louder from day to day, each becoming clearer and better differentiated. And the sources located easily now.

Either with pricked, semi-pricked or floppy ears, dogs have a fantastic sense of hearing (and an excellent understanding for the spoken word). This doesn't happen from birth because their auditory canals are still closed at that point. It's not before the third week of life that the skin wrinkles start to stretch and to open up, so that air molecules and therefore sound waves can be transmitted.

Nevertheless, there is no absolute radio silence in the acoustic nerve of a newborn dog. If, for example, an alarm clock turns on, directly beside the whelping box, the sound waves caused by that noise are enough to set the puppies' heads vibrating. At this point, the sound waves are transmitted via so-called bone conduction directly to the hearing organ in the inner ear, and produce the auditory perception there. Such contact vibrations can even directly stimulate the ossicles in the middle ear – without passing the eardrum – to thus reach the vestibular apparatus in the inner ear. What influence such environmental stimuli really has on the puppy is unexplored so far. It's assumed that they contribute to the socialisation, if not appearing too often and too intense, and thus strengthen the puppy's security in the environment.

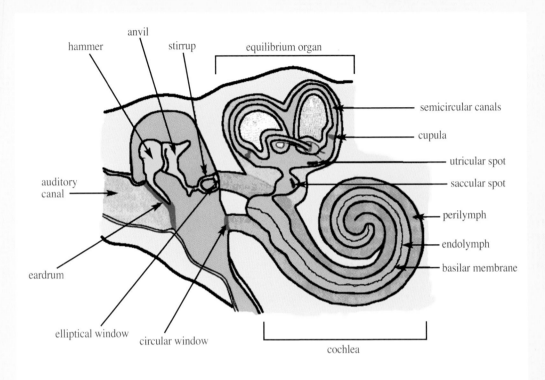

The dog's ear.

The structure of the ear

The dog's hearing organ consists of the external (outer), the middle and the inner ear. The outer ear consists of the auricle and the conspicuously long auditory canal, covered with a mucous membrane. The auditory canal is bordered by a white, bright membrane at its inner end, the eardrum. Then follows the middle ear, a cavity filled with air in which so-called ossicles are lined up looking something like a pearl necklace. This cavity, that is also called the tympanic cavity, is connected to the throat with a narrow tube (Eustachian tube) and is ventilated when swallowing. The bony tympanic cavity is connected to the inner ear and its auditory sensory cells via two openings (the upper elliptical window and, located below, the circular window). It's this inner area of the ear, called the labyrinth – on average only measuring 12 millimetres long – that is the dog's real hearing organ (organ of corti), wherein the dog's equilibrium organ is located, and with which it controls its position and keeps itself stable.

The dog's sense of hearing is very watchful as it almost never gets tired. It can perceive softer and higher tones than ours and it can clearly distinguish them. It's also generally better at locating sound sources.

The sound's journey through the dog's ear

Sound develops when, for example, freely moving molecules in the air are set vibrating. With these molecules transmitting their kinetic energy in the form of pressure variations to the neighbouring molecules, the sound spreads in the form of waves. That is when the actual hearing begins. The way in which the eardrum moves, due to the impact of sound, already contains important details of

the overall acoustic information that later reaches the brain via the acoustic nerves.

Therefore, the force of the deflection of the membrane depends on the intensity of the pressure variation, and, therefore, on the amplitude of the sound waves. The greater their amplitude, the stronger the deflection – and therefore the louder the perceived sound event. How often the eardrum moves back and forth depends on the number of pressure variations and thus the frequency of the sound waves. The higher the frequency, the more often it moves back and forth, and the higher the tone that the dog finally perceives. Additionally, different parts of the dog's eardrum, that on average measures 46 square millimetres, can also move back and forth independently from each other and can thus transmit information that is contained, for example, in the form of the appearing sound waves.

This thin membrane has to be quite supple to be that flexible. The earwax provides the necessary lubricant. If there is too much earwax, the auditory capacity declines, as thick layers of earwax on the eardrum make it inflexible and are not of any help for the transmission of sound waves. The eardrum also becomes inflexible if it's inflamed or perforated. But a healthy eardrum membrane is not only a guarantee for a good transportation of sound waves. It's also very important for the health of the middle and inner ear, since micro organisms such as bacteria, viruses and yeast fungi can enter via holes and, if the worst comes to the worst, lead to a total loss of the sense of hearing, that in turn weakens the dog's ability to orientate.

The auricle's job

Sound normally spreads linearly, but it can be diverted or reflected by massive obstacles. Different warm air layers close to the earth, or changed weather conditions can lead to the sound waves being refracted and perceived differently. For example, the dog can hear much better with the wind, than against it. With dense fog, everything sounds dull. One should necessarily account for this when training the dog. With the development of large, funnel-shaped external ears, Mother Nature has created a great instrument, in order to increase the acoustic perception, by making use of those qualities of sound. Thus the naturally pricked ears are located as large collection funnels at the side of the dog's head and collect even the slightest sounds that can be of importance to the ability to orientate.

The auricles are designed to reflect even the sound waves that reach the outer edges and to transmit them inwards, thereby the received sound is increasingly bundled together and therefore becomes more intense. This is also assisted by the fine hair that covers the inside of the outer ears – and especially by numerous wavy-shaped elevations, the so-called ear cartilage. These cartilage folds can also be found far inside the ear. They contribute to the sound finally reaching the eardrum by passing the outer auditory canal without losing almost any of its intensity.

The dog's very long auditory canal, with its bend typically located halfway, can even increase the transmission of the sound to a certain degree, as the auditory canal is also

The very virtuoso movements of the dog's ears are not only serve to perceive of sound, but also used for communication.

a flexible structure with a resonance frequency of roughly 4 kilohertz.

That means that a sound wave in exactly this frequency area can be transmitted especially well and can be perceived by the dog very clearly. But the dog's large auricles, with their complex cartilage structures, can do much more than just collect and bundle sound waves, they can also specifically aim at a sound source. With the 17 highly efficient muscles that steer their flexibility, they

In dogs with floppy ears, when inserting drops, especially, the auditory canal should be bent carefully.

The auricles change the sound of a sound event – thus the dog receives additional information about whether the sound approaches the ear from the front or from the back.

can take up a variety of positions and can scan the environment for interesting sounds like a directional microphone.

As dogs can move their auricles independently from each other, they are able to scan their environment inch-perfectly and, therefore, perceive sounds from just one direction and increase them, or to ignore disturbing sounds coming from other directions. Therefore, a defined sound source can be located.

It's interesting that the ability to hear of dogs with floppy ears is hardly worse than that of dogs with pricked ears. They are almost as good at locating sounds – only rarely do they need a measurable sound intensity. Lappets, which are hanging over the auditory canal, admittedly do deaden the sound so that noises coming from a certain direction appear to be a bit softer. Nevertheless, it's obvious when dogs with floppy ears hold their head close to the ground when sniffing around, that sufficient (and sometimes maybe even more or louder) sound information from the ground or the nearby areas reaches the auditory canal better than with dogs with pricked or tipped ears.

As far as the registration of different depths of tones is concerned, floppy ears nevertheless seem to have a disadvantage: Dachshunds, at any rate, whose hanging ears have temporarily been tied to the head, were able to perceive clearly higher tones than usual. It needn't be feared, however, that this fact involves any loss of quality of life or the ability to work for those four-legged floppy-eared animals, as their excellent ability to hear significantly outstrips even ours.

Tiny bones help dogs to hear

Dogs are able to recognise even the slightest sound and they manage to retrieve various information from every sound. They easily perceive minimal changes of the tone pitch or differences in volume as well as different samples or even pitches. Three tiny bones in the middle ear support are the reason.

The descriptive names of those minor bones are hammer, anvil and stirrup. With a length of just 10, 4 and 2 millimetres, respectively, they are responsible for leading the sound energy from the eardrum to the elliptical window in the inner ear. To fulfil this task, all three of them are flexibly connected. Additionally, the hammer, located close to the eardrum, is directly connected to the eardrum with its little handle. The stirrup, closest to the inner ear, lies on the bony ring to the inner ear, the elliptical window. A direct mechanic connection between the eardrum and the passage to the inner ear is established – and thereby the possibility of a detailed transmission of the sound energy from the auricle to the inner ear.

Without this extravagant construction, the sound waves couldn't even reach the inner ear, they would simply bounce off the elliptical window. The reason for that is the different densities of air and liquids. It's in the elliptical window where the sound wave, which has been transmitted in the air so far, directly meets a liquid medium, the so-called perilymph. The dainty ossicles now prevent this almost complete reflection of the sound energy, because due to the different sizes of the eardrum and the stirrup, with their special construction and their tiny size, the pressure is being increased during the transmission. Therefore a better transmission of the sound information is guaranteed, even across resistance levels.

If the dog suffers from an infection of the middle ear (because, for instance, the mucous membrane that covers the tympanic cavity and the ossicles is inflamed) its ability to hear decreases. Hammer, anvil and stirrup are then limited in their flexibility, and so their transmission performance declines.

Besides the ossicles, the middle ear consists of two muscles that conduct an adaptation to different volumes by, for instance, changing the tension of the eardrum or the flexible connection between the ossicles. On the one hand the transmission of soft sound is therefore increased, on the other hand the transmission of loud sounds in decreased. The assumption that those muscles protect the dog's ear from too loud sound events is rather improbable. It simply takes too long until their action comes into effect, let's say after a bang.

It's rather probable that the muscles of the middle ear prevent the joints of the filigree ossicles clattering, especially with the transmission of very high frequencies. Well-founded proof of this doesn't exist.

About sound waves and frequencies

Unlike light, with sound one speaks of the number of vibrations per second, called frequency (unit: hertz, abbreviated Hz), not of wavelengths. Young, healthy people can perceive sound within a frequency range of about 16 to 20,000 vibrations per second at the most (16 hertz to 20 kilohertz [kHz]at the most). With dogs, the range is much wider as they also perceive sound in the high frequency range, the ultrasound. Dogs can pretty definitely hear all frequencies between 30 hertz and 64 kilohertz. It's unlikely that values of almost 100 kilohertz, measured with some individuals, can be confirmed for all dogs. The same applies to the assumption that not only some breeds, but actually all dogs, can perceive sounds within the low frequency range, the infrasound.

Although there are clues for the assumption that the dogs' ability to hear (unlike the majority of the mammals) does not depend on their height, today it's assumed that smaller dogs can perceive higher tones than their larger congeners. This is also due to their skull anatomy and the very light ossicles that guarantee a very good transmission adjustment to high sound frequencies. Large dogs, on the other hand, should be able to perceive much lower tones than small dogs (due especially to their enlarged middle ear volume). Single species can even perceive frequencies far below our sound waves.

Such low-frequency sound waves are, for example, produced by surf, by the wind at mountain ridges or by industry works. They spread, totally differently from ultrasound, across huge distances without almost any loss in intensity. Therefore, infrasound is an ideal signal for distance orientation, for example, when a dog has to find its way home from far away. Avalanches setting off, imminent earthquakes or threatening hurricanes cause the same clear low-frequency sounds, by which certain dogs can acoustically perceive the threatening disaster long before we can.

Different points of view also exist when it comes to the question about which frequency range the dog's ear reacts most sensitively within. All in all, this range seems to be much wider than that of the human ear with 500 hertz to 4 kilohertz. Additionally, it comprises much higher frequencies. This enlarged frequency range of the dog is assumed to range from 1 to 16 kilohertz. This enlargement significantly contributes to the fact that dogs have a much better sense of hearing than we do. Because, especially within this maximum sensitivity range, much softer sounds can still be perceived and their frequencies can lie together much more closely, and can still be perceived as different tones.

Dogs achieve perfect results in this frequency range when it comes to the analysis of different pitches. Yes, they even have perfect hearing when they differentiate sounds that only differ from each other by an eighth tone. They can perceive minimal differences in volumes within this frequency range that we can no longer perceive.

A sound that dogs can perceive and differentiate, even from a distance of 400 metres, can only be perceived by us when it's no longer further away than 100 metres. Does it still surprise us then that our dog runs to the garden gate to await its master, when the master's wife does not even know that he will shortly arrive?

Their ability to estimate distances, in particular, benefits from this exact analysis of acoustic signals, as it mainly depends on the shift of the frequency spectrum that reaches the ear from different sound source distances.

As high frequencies are muffled more than low frequencies when being transmitted, the sound that crosses a larger distance contains fewer proportions of high frequencies than a sound that only crossed a short distance.

High tones don't travel very far. Nevertheless, with their highly sensitive ears, it' easy for dogs to perceive the high-frequency squeaks of a mouse in her hiding place in the ground. Our four-legged companions can also easily hear the dog whistles with their high sound frequencies of roughly 25 kilohertz, that we perceive to be soundless.

Additionally, it's much softer. As dogs can easily perceive all these deviations, even the slightest, it's not surprising that they can measure distances that precisely, especially with the help of acoustic signals.

The cochlea in the inner ear

When the sound waves have crossed the resistance level from the middle ear to the inner ear, they reach a spiralled canal of approximately 30 millimetres: the cochlea. The cochlea is triple winding; the human cochlea has half a winding less. This cochlea contains three staggered tubes, filled with liquid, within which the sound waves are transmitted. The middle tube is filled with a viscous liquid which contains high amounts of potassium (called endolymph) – and two neighbouring tubes that contain a very sodium-rich liquid (called perilymph) (see the diagram at the beginning of the chapter).

The upper perilymph tube has an elliptical window at its beginning and extends to the top of the cochlea, where it passes into the lower perilymph tube, which in turn ends at the wall of the tympanic cavity at a thin membrane, the circular window. This membrane serves to balance the shift in volume that is caused by the vibration within the liquid in the elliptical window. If a sound wave hits the eardrum, the stirrup, following the rhythm of the vibrations, pushes into the upper liquid, whose content passes on the shock wave as far as it reaches, and beats out the circular window.

The wave motions do, of course, not remain limited to the two perilymph tubes, but also extend to the centrally located endolymph tube. Different elastic ligaments, which are also moved by the vibration, are stretched there; one of them is the so-called basilar membrane. The auditory sensory cells are located on this basilar membrane, close to each other and embedded in supportive cells. The dog supposedly has roughly 20,000 of these auditory sensory cells per ear, each of them with an approximate thickness of 0.2 millimetres, a length of 0.5 millimetres and shapes that vary from one like a cylinder to one like a pear. Similarly to the olfactory sensory cells, these sensory cells have numerous little hairs (cilia) at their front end, which is why they are also called hair cells. And as is known from the olfactory cells, these very fine projections fulfil an important role in excitation.

Directly at their outer edges, another colloidal membrane structure is located, which – and this is crucial for the reaction – is located at a slightly different point than the basilar membrane. When sound waves are received and the elliptical window experiences differences in pressure and therefore shifts in the head of liquid, these two membranes shift as well and start to move from one side to the other. Now the cilia are being bent. It's this specific stimulus that the sensory cells are so desperately waiting for. Finally the acoustic information, namely the mechanical energy of the sound waves, can be transformed into electrical energy and can be transmitted, via the auditory pathway, to the brain.

Every detail of how the absorption of stimuli takes place and how, because of that, a receptor and finally an action potential arises is extremely complicated and would not be of further interest here. Two things are important at this point: firstly, that the dog's cilia react extremely fast (within an incredible 0.04 milliseconds) to even the slightest mechanical influence, they can thus be stimulated by the tiniest sound stimuli.

The special adjustments of the dog's ear make it very efficient. The uniquely constructed auricle contributes to this as well as the ossicles, the cochlea and the central processing areas.

With very high volumes, for example a loud engine sound, the basilar membrane vibrates by roughly 1 micrometer; with soft sounds, as at our threshold of hearing, it vibrates by less than 1 nanometre.

And secondly, that the cilia, as secondary sensory cells, do not produce their own nerve fibres on which the electric signals can be transmitted – and that they therefore need a supply through other nerve fibres. These nerve fibres can in turn drastically influence the behaviour of the cilia.

It could be said that they exist in two versions. One version is located on the cilia, receives information there and then sends it to the central nervous system in the auditory cortex via the auditory pathway. The other version in fact borders to the cilia, but it does not retrieve its information from those receptor cells, but from the brain cells of the dog. The exciting effect of this so-called afferent (targeting the brain) or efferent (coming from the brain) nerve supply is that the auditory sensory cells do not only supply the dog's central nervous system with information, but also receive information from there themselves. Such impulses can have a hindering or an exciting effect and can be based on acoustic information received earlier, or on totally different stimuli from the brain, or the current motivational situation of the animal.

If the dog is in a watchful state, for example, this can increase the sensibility of just some cilia or all of the cilia. Indifference, distraction and general tiredness can decrease their reaction threshold. The interactions are quite manifold and depend on the experience of each animal. In any case, they significantly contribute to the fact that dogs can, for example, sleep even surrounded by noise and can simultaneously be very watchful of very specific, relevant acoustic events. Listening and ignoring: with this principle, our dogs manage to filter specific sounds and prioritise certain tones out of a sound cocktail, even when these sounds are less strongly developed than their acoustic surrounding.

Although dogears are so much more sensitive than human ears, dogs seem to be much less bothered by constant noise (that would take some of us to the brink of despair).

This was the result of measurements of physiological stress indicators such as pulse, blood pressure and cortisol content in the blood of the animals. The typical selection behaviour of the dogs' ear seems to contribute to this. But despite all survey results: we should not expect too much of our dogs in this respect!

Perception of tone pitch and volume

The deflection that the basilar membrane experiences through the received shock wave is pretty strange and, obviously, also depends on its width, thickness and flexibility. This so-called travelling wave, arising from the elliptical window, passes the cochlea as a wave on a horizontally held rope, which is fixed at one end. Thus far, this behaviour hasn't been completely understood. In any case, it is clear that a maximum deflection always develops at a certain spot of the basilar membrane – and therefore a creation of the local auditory sensory cells also takes place. Where exactly this maximum deflection develops depends on the frequency of the sound wave: the higher the sound frequency, the closer it is to the stirrup – and the lower the frequency, the further it takes place in the direction of the top of the cochlea.

Thus the frequency of the sound stimuli is coded on the basilar membrane dependent on the location, which means that each pitch is allocated to a specific location of the endolymph tube.

The more densely the receptors are located there, the more precise can the frequency analysis and therefore the differentiation of various tone pitches be. The cilia that are stimulated by high tones seem to react especially selectively. Also this behaviour obviously contributes to the fact that dogs can differentiate such high-frequency sound events that precisely.

At the same time as the frequency, the intensity of the perceived sound is registered. The louder the sound, the more often the nerve fibres, leading to the respective cilia, "shoot" and the more neighbouring cells are involved in the reaction. The chronological course of such an impulse pattern reflects the duration of the sound event and the pauses between them.

The fact that dogs can, on the one hand, perceive much softer sounds than we can (up to four times softer) and, on the other hand,

Within the range of the highest octave, which human beings can only just perceive, dogs only need a thousandth part of the sound energy that we need for the same hearing experience.

Hissing sounds, with their high frequencies, normally attract the dog's attention much faster than a long lasting growl. With mysterious whispering, one can quickly bring a dog that is familiar to human behaviour, out of its shell.

have a much better spatial resolution for acoustic stimuli, cannot be explained by any conspicuous anatomy or the function of the sensory cells. It's rather the much better construction of their external and middle ear and the especially extravagant structure of their so-called ascending auditory pathway, as well as the auditory cortex in the cerebrum, whose nerve cells make an especially sharp contrast possible, and are responsible for the fine perception.

The good memory for sound events is also admirable. Dogs can, for example, memorise sound patterns and tone sequences, even tone pitches, for years – and can fall back on this detailed information when required. Additionally, they have a fast working, good sense of hearing. That means they can differentiate series of acoustic impulses even when they come thick and fast. With human beings, very fast impulse sequences melt into one single hearing experience significantly earlier. Of course, this high temporal resolution also enables dogs to perceive and to decipher sounds extremely fast.

Dogs can perceive two sound sources, placed 5 metres away from them, as two single sound sources, even when they are only 15 centimetres apart from each other.

Sound localisation

When hunting, a fast and differentiated sense of hearing is also essential. The excellent directivity of the auricle plays an important part here. Therefore to precisely locate a sound source within a split second is an easy thing for dogs to do.

Even with only one ear, sound localisation is possible. Admittedly not over long distances or with very weak sound events, but even so, one-sidedly deaf dogs (not dogs that were born deaf) can manage to establish a kind of spatial hearing with the help of the auricle of their perfectly functioning ear.

"Paulchen, come here!" – Dogs can locate a sound source 10 times better than we can.

The bulges and wrinkles of the auricle, that are bent upwards and downwards, refract and reflect the different frequencies of a mixture of sounds dependent on the incidence direction in a characteristic way. This leads to typical changes in the transmission to the eardrum. The brain retrieves important information concerning the direction of the sound from these changes. Also, healthy ears make use of this auricular skill when rapidly recognising whether a sound source is located in front or behind them. The auricles don't even have to move to do that!

If dogs adjust their ears to the source of a sound, the locating, of course, becomes much more precise. Both ears then receive different sound information which the central nervous system finally turns into the spatial impression. Thus the sound reaches the ear that is turned away from the sound source milliseconds later than the ear turned towards the source. Additionally, the sound is slightly softer on the side that is turned away. Incidentally, it gets softer the higher the sound frequency is, as the head or the air, respectively, deaden higher tones much more than the lower ones.

Due to this so-called transmission time, or rather level difference, the dog's sound sensitive nerve cells in the brain determine the direction from which the sound reaches the ear. Or they give further instructions to, for example, the muscles of its auricle or its neck if the information is not yet sufficient for precise localisation. This information is transmitted via a complicated network constructed of nerve fibres. The dog then turns its head to change and to determine the angle of incidence of the sound, to establish from which direction the sounds gets respectively louder or quieter, Thus its auditory pathway finds complete clarity.

The dog only needs time differences of 10 microseconds – meaning a 100,000th part of a second – to find out from which direction the sound is received – or in other words, only a single degree.

We need between 3-10 degrees to locate a sound, this corresponds to a sound time difference of 30 to 100 microseconds.

The equilibrium organ

Another highly sensitive sense organ within its inner ear is essential for the dog's orientation in space: the equilibrium organ or vestibular organ. It's located directly beside the cochlea and functions as a rotational organ, as well as a translation organ. So-called semicircular canals register the rotational acceleration of the head. Macula cells on the other hand, register its deviation from the vertical.

Both receptor structures transmit impulses through the so-called vestibularis nerve. This is a nerve cell complex in the dog's brain that sends information to, for example, the hind brain, the area in the brain that is responsible for the direction of the fine motor skills for controlled movements. There are also nerve connections, starting at this complex, leading to the skeletal muscles and the muscles of the eyes, via which regulatory impulses are sent to the so-called postural motor system. Thus it's guaranteed that suitable balancing movements are conducted within a split second, when the position of the head or movement of the eyes, that stabilise the dog's system, are changed. These reactions, referred to as startle and postural reflex, make certain that dogs don't lose their equilibrium, even in the most difficult movement situations. They also ensure that they always keep an eye on their environment, despite movements of the head or the body when walking, running or jumping, as a perfect optic orientation is only possible with fixation of the visual field.

If a dog suffers from a bacterial or viral affection of the inner ear, besides the ability to hear, the performance of the sense of balance is also decreased.

Thus, sick animals stumble or suddenly fall to the side. They may constantly keep their head lop-sided and their eyeballs perform un-coordinated movements or twitch heavily. Also, when dogs are swimming, they experience major co-ordination problems. It's the close spatial relation of both sense organs that is responsible for such disturbances and which makes a direct exchange of liquids, and therefore potential pathogens, possible, as not only is the cochlea filled with en-dolymph, but so are the hollows within the equilibrium organ.

The dog's equilibrium organ consists of three circularly bent tubes filled with liquid: the semi-circular canals. All three of them are positioned at a 90-degree angle to each other. One is horizontal, the two others are positioned vertically to the horizontal one – in the same way as two walls are positioned to the ceiling of a room (see the illustration on page 83). Due to this special arrangement, it's possible to register all rotational move-ments, no matter which space axis they fol-low. Within the inside of each semi-circular canal, there is a colloidal barrier, the cupu-la. There are sensory cells rising into the cupula that are stuck directly at the oppos-ing wall of the canal. As with the cochlea, they belong to the secondary sensory cells and just like them; they have cilia at their outer ends, which significantly contribute to the stimulation. If the dog, for example, turns its head, the semi-circular canals move as well. The endolymph they are filled with cannot follow this movement immediately,

nevertheless, due to its inertia. As a result of this delayed reaction, a flow within the tube is created, that in turn bends the cupula and, therefore, the cilia. The receptor cells in turn respond to this stimulus, and this finally leads to an impulse transmission via the nerve fibres leading to the brain.

As one semi-circular canal carries cilia of different kinds and sizes (the tiny hair get longer from one end to the other), the re-ceptors reach a directional sensitivity that enables them to recognise whether move-ment of their cilia takes place from left to right or vice versa. And it's exactly this in-formation that the semi-circular canals need to trigger compensational movements of the eyes or the body.

The macula cells, that are located below its semicircular canals in a kind of vestibule, guarantee the dog's body is kept upright. Two of them can be found in each ear: they are called the saccular spot and utricular spot. Also, these structures that support the sense of balance carry direction-sensitive sensory cells with cilia, that dip into a colloidal lay-er. Within this colloidal layer, there are cal-cite crystals that have a higher specific den-sity than the surrounding medium. This different density causes movements of the head, with different forces, to influence the endolymph on the one hand, and the calcite-containing colloidal layer on the other hand. As a result of this, the colloidal layer slides a little over the layer of sensory cells, which in turn causes the cilia to be bent and leads to the production of nerve impulses.

The crucial stimulus for the macula cells is gravity, whereas the cilia on the saccular

Moving confidently on an expanse of rubble is no problem, even for the largest of dogs, thanks to its excellent sense of balance.

How the hearing performance changes

As soon as the auditory canals have completely opened up after roughly three weeks, the acoustic impressions of the dog become more differentiated from day to day. From roughly 6 months up to the middle years, its auditory performance basically stays the same, after that, it constantly deteriorates. At first, it's only the very high frequencies that the elderly dog can't perceive any more. Later, it's also the lower ones. As it gets older, the dog, therefore, needs louder sound sources to be able to clearly recognise them. Very old dogs often even turn completely deaf.

The age-related deterioration of hearing takes place, in most cases, very slowly, so that the dogs have the chance to adjust themselves to the increasing loss of their abilities by using other senses like, for example, their nose much more when orientating. But if the hearing completely fails suddenly, as a result of an infectious disease, for example, the dog doesn't have any time for those adjustments. This is, of course, one of the reasons why dogs often react very nervously and show serious orientation and even movement dysfunctions in such cases. To come to terms with this sudden change, such animals have, nevertheless, to start learning to completely rely on their remaining senses. The owners can support them by a communication that is now increasingly based on clear hand signals and close body contact. At least the communication with the human being can thus be guaranteed and one can give the dog back a little bit of its security. However, the loss of

spot mainly respond to vertical accelerations, and the sensory cells on the utricular spot are mainly activated by horizontal acceleration.

Like their close relatives, the wolves, dogs can get much more out of sounds and even music, and the loss of their hearing ability can have dramatic consequences on their well-being.

hearing performance represents a drastic deterioration in its quality of life, especially for a young animal. That's why such a loss has to be avoided at all costs, not only with good health care and through regular inoculations, but also through careful breeding because unfortunately, there are genetic dispositions, like the ones for less pigmentation of the hair, that favour the failure of the sensory system (especially in the area of their cochlea) and that are otherwise passed on unhindered from generation to generation.

Breeds that carry the so-called spotting gene in their genotype, as well as those with the merle gene, are mainly affected by such sensory defects.

With this kind of dog, extreme difficulties (as well as one sided or total deafness) appear much more often than with other breeds. Even with heterozygote merle carrier (and therefore with animals who have this gene in their genotype), losses of hearing are registered much more often, as well as measurable impairments of the vision.

With a special hearing test, the audiometric test, a (threatening) loss of hearing can be diagnosed beyond doubt in puppies of five weeks. The electric activities that arise as a result of an auditory stimulus in the cochlea, as well as in the auditory nerve and the brain, can be easily registered with tiny electrodes that are relatively painlessly pinched into the scalp of the puppy. Especially with deafness or the loss of hearing of only one ear, most of the time observations of behaviour don't provide a clear result, although it can give hints of a hearing disorder.

Deaf dogs, for example, treat their play companions much more roughly than dogs that can hear. They simply lack the feedback of the soft protest whimpering of the other dogs. Deaf dogs also bark much louder than their healthy peers – the reason is the missing so-called Lombard's voice reflex, that adjusts the sound of the voice, in this case the bark, via a feedback of the noise level. Of course, the reaction to auditory stimuli is also significantly changed and can be recognised by close observation.

Despite these indications, misinterpretation, that makes the judgement more difficult, can creep in with the use of behaviour analysis. As pack animals, dogs orientate by their social partners. It can, for example,

happen that a deaf puppy's behaviour is not at all odd in the beginning, as he always follows its littermates to a (soft) sound source. What does the puppy really perceive, however, when we loudly clap our hands or stamp our foot on the ground? Is it really the acoustic stimulus or does the puppy maybe react to the triggered vibrations with its sense of touch? Electro diagnostic examinations provide clarity, as they are objective and clear.

Colour pigments influence the hearing

Why, we ask ourselves, are dogs with special sorts of lesser pigmentation of their hair more frequently affected by hearing or optic disorders? The answer is equally simple and appalling: It's because of the close evolutionary relationship of certain cells in their body (those that are responsible for the pigmentation of the hair and that control the development of nerve structures) and their joint influence through certain genes.

The colour of skin and hair is achieved by melanin pigments that in turn are produced by special cells, the melanocytes. The melanocytes are contained in the so-called neural crest that is a basic structure from which all cells of the central nervous system (CNS) and its so-called appendix organs originate, for example the dog's eyes and ears. If pathogen changes happen within this common structure during the embryonic development, all components can be equally affected.

Probably, it's the genes, in particular, that are responsible for the special colour charac-

Besides the changed hair or eye colour, certain genes can cause significant, irreversible functional losses of the dog's auditory sensory cells. This puppy is having an audiometric test to ensure its hearing works perfectly.

teristics that can intervene negatively into the development of such dog breeds at this stage. They definitely do intervene, at the latest, on the level of the function of the auditory sensory cells. There, also, the melanin producing cells, as well as the merle and spotting gene, play a crucial part. Melanocytes can not only be found in the skin, mucous membranes and hair of the dog, but they can also be found in great numbers in its optic and acoustic system, as well as in its equilibrium organ and in certain areas of its central nervous system.

In the auditory system, for example, the melanocytes contribute to the stabilisation of the potassium level of the endolymph. A high concentration of this mineral is the condition for the functionality of the cilia of the cochlea. If the concentration permanently falls below a crucial value, at the worst, this leads to a decline of all sensory cells and therefore to the loss of hearing performance.

What does all this have to do with the lesser pigmentation genes? These genes intervene directly into the potassium control process by, on the one hand, influencing the melanocytes in their effect and, on the other hand, suppressing their sufficient production. Significant dysfunctions in the mineral balance of the inner ear are the disastrous consequences.

Despite intensive research, the hereditary process that forms the basis of this effect has not so far been deciphered. One assumes that there are complex reasons behind all this. One indication is that not all animals that have such genes in their genotype are equally affected by sensory defects. As long as there are no ultimate results about the respective heredity processes, besides the careful breeding, there's only the audiometry to identify affected dogs early enough and to exclude them from the breeding programme, as dogs that are deaf on one side often behave normally and are therefore not recognised at risk takers.

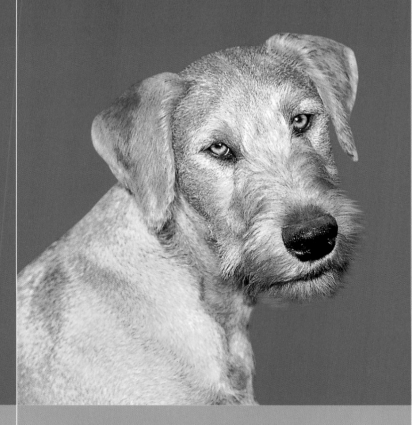

There is nothing supernatural

Dogs astonish us time and again with their ability to perceive things that we don't have the faintest idea of at that moment. There are, however, no supernatural capabilities of our four-legged companions at the bottom of this, the reason is simply the incredibly high sensitivity of their sense system.

As we cannot comprehend the complex dog's sense world even with the liveliest imagination, we tend to compare this ability with something psychic.

In honesty, we should confess that the sensory abilities of dogs have not been inspected in every single detail yet, and that they are surely still keeping exciting secrets hidden. It should also lead us to the realisation that these abilities are not supernatural, but simply due to a purely material basis – to anatomic and physiological factors that are concrete and above all conceivable.

Therefore, it's their incredibly well developed sense of timing that enables them to assess when their master is going to be home. This sensibility, of course, has a totally real source in the so-called body clock that amongst other things controls numerous processes in the dog's body besides the sense of time. (By the way, the body clock is located in the area of the hypothalamus, in the dog's diencephalon, and consists of a complex of nerve cells, the so-called suprachiasmatic nucleus, – SCN.)

If such an excellent sense of time is now combined with a sense of hearing and touch that can perceive even the softest sounds, the result is clear: the dog hears and feels the master's arrival long before the master's wife knows that he is about to arrive – without any supernatural powers!

With their extremely sensitive sense of hearing, they can register additionally even the softest crunch and the extremely quiet cracking sounds that arise within the ground, when the pressure builds up, shortly before an imminent earthquake. The dogs can perceive this much earlier than we can –they can even perceive it long before measurement instruments react for the first time.

Also the infrared detectors, that are probably located on the dog's nose leather, provide their owner with important information.

Avalanche rescue dogs, for example, know whether a victim, buried under the snow, is still alive or already dead. As specific temperature receptors, these sensors seem to react with special sensitivity to the slightest differences in thermal radiation.

Dogs also have a well-developed electric sensibility, as they are able to perceive electricity and to react to electromagnetic fields. In particular, their millions of tiny body hairs with sensitive touch receptors can transmit those reactions that are induced by the field impact – for example in the form of slightest vibrations of the hair. But dogs can not only feel electric, magnetic or electromagnetic fields, they even seem to be able to perceive static magnetic fields of the earth. Magnetic sediments in their head (probably the recently discovered traces of iron in their nose) should enable the animals to recognise changes in the magnetic field and to adjust their behaviour according to them. Besides the perception of ultrasound, this is an additional explanation for their brilliant ability to find their way home, with which certain dogs have always been puzzling mankind.

And last but not least, there's the astonishing sensitivity with which our dogs react to our unconscious signals and with which they register our bearing, gesture, mood and changed body odours. Out of all the different messages, they receive a detailed impression of how we feel or what we are about to do next. All the dog's super senses play together here: smelling as well as hearing, seeing and touching – nothing more!

Our dogs' world is, admittedly, less colourful and less optically detailed than ours is, but it's much richer in smells and brighter. Additionally, dogs hear more and louder sounds and they perceive movements much faster. They also perceive things that we barely feel or don't feel at all, due to our less sensitive sense organs. How nice, that they nevertheless get involved with us ...

When two social kinds get together

As very social living beings, dogs have developed multi-faceted and pretty clear ways of communicating that avoid misunderstandings among their peers, to a great extent, (and with us human beings). Whether on an optic, acoustic, tactile or olfactory level, most of the time they send their signals all too clearly and often also typically. For communication across large distances, dogs mainly use acoustic and optic signals, for close and finer communication, they mostly rely on smells and the tactile orientation. And therefore it's no surprise that it's especially the touch and olfactory sensory cells that start working first in a puppy with its tiny radius of action. It's also those senses that tend to keep working without restriction all through a dog's life – and are often the only means left to us to communicate with our favourite pet.

The dog's vocabulary

Dogs tell us their personal business via very discriminated kinds of barking. Furthermore, they can also listen to our acoustic expressions and interpret them. The passive vocabulary of a guide dog, for example, comprises roughly 80 words. The so-called comprehension vocabulary is much more comprehensive with single genius dogs. Nevertheless, without any eye or body contact, just the spoken word, dogs can probably only understand up to 6 words. This means they always make use of other information besides the spoken word (timbre, melodies). This information consists of our mimic signals, as well as of our gestures, or our moods. Every dog tries to discover as many of these hints as possible by closely watching its owner. The dog's ability for this depends on its genes, on the one hand, and on how often the owner involves the dog and talks to him, on the other. Nevertheless, every dog, disregarding its cleverness, has difficulties in associating a certain action or a certain item with a defined word. A high motivation, a lot of praise and treats are the only things that work here.

One should be prepared for the dog to insidiously lose its sensory skills and we should be able to support our four-legged companion with respective touch stimuli in the daily routine. Especially with a very old dog, such symptoms are inevitable because, besides the limitations in terms of receptor cells (including its sense of balance), the dog's brain gradually loses mass and weight. With a medium sized dog, it can amount to an annual decrease of roughly 2-4 per cent after the fourth year. This inevitably leads to a constant decrease of the synaptic control centres; in addition, the speed with which signals are transmitted and processed slows down. With a 12-year-old dog, the rate of the nerve conduction only equals a fourth of the speed of a 4-year-old dog.

If our elderly dog doesn't react that promptly anymore when getting older; if it stumbles from time to time or suddenly shows unusual actions, we should have sympathy for this and should try to adjust our own behaviour to the changed circumstances as much as possible. Our old companion really deserves this consideration – as he himself has always been determined to find a common conversation basis with us, his oh so different friends. This process had already started on its evolutionary way from wolf to dog.

The comparison of different dog breeds revealed that the dog's sensory performance has lost some accuracy, in general, but some parts of its cerebrum have gained size and complexity while adjusting to its changing environment. The number of photoreceptors in the dog's retina, for example, as well as the ganglion cell and nerve fibre density is measurably smaller and so is the eardrum. Furthermore, a significant decrease in certain central processing areas of sensory stimuli can be registered, for example in the visual cortex or the telencephalon.

These are all changes that account for the decreased performance of dogs only in a sensory way. The auditory cortex and, thus, the comprehension of sounds are, in contrast, no less developed than those in wolves. Its so-called projection areas in the ascending auditory canal have even grown. This says something for the prime importance of this special sense quality in the successful communication between dog and human.

In contrast to many of its other subtle optic signals, simply lost during its development (because they were not understood by the human being and thus didn't provide a survival advantage for the dog), acoustic communication became more and more important. Not least because of this, the dog's vocal expression is much more differentiated than that of wolves. Additionally, it proved to be favourable for the dogs to live as close as possible together with this strange species of human being.

This close interaction with a different species made them to do one thing: they had to develop higher psychological performances. And thus the dogs' so-called association areas in the cerebral cortex have significantly grown, despite a relative decrease in their cerebral matter in comparison with their ancestor, the wolf. These are areas in the brain in which information that is registered via the single sensory canals is put together and evaluated, and – what has even further-reaching consequences – where what is generally called understanding is produced; namely the understanding of coherences and their meaning.

Via those anatomical and physiological changes in the dog's brain, the basis was established for an inter-species communication and for the living together of two such different species as dogs and humans simply are. At the same time, this provided the chance for the development of an inimitably good empathy that enables our friends to communicate with us so overwhelmingly well, despite their completely different sensory world.

Let's enjoy this unique company – even in such a sorrowful moment when our companion closes its inquiring eyes for ever: it will remain an indelible experience.

Literature

Adams, D.R./Wiekamp, M.D.
The canine vomeronasal organ
Journal of Anatomy, 138, 771-784, 1984

Anholt, R.R.H.
Primary events in olfactory reception
Trends in Biochemical Science, Vol. 12, 58-62, 1987

Baker, M.A.
Rapid brain cooling in exercising dogs
Scinece, Vol. 195, 781-783, 1977

Von Békésy, G.
Olfactory analogue to directional hearing
Journal of Applied Physiology 19, 369-373, 1964

Berlin, Ch.I.
Hemispheric asymmetry in auditory tasks
Academic Press, 1977

Breipohl, W. (ed.)
Olfaction an endocrine regulation
London: IRL Press, 1982

Bulanda, S./Luther, L.
Ready! A step-by-step guide for
training the search and rescue dog
Doral Publishing, 1995

Bulanda, S.
Ready to serve, ready to save:
Strategies of real-life search and rescue missions
Doral Publishing, 1999

Bulanda, S.
Scenting on the wind: scent work for hunting dogs
Doral Publishing, 2003

Doty, R.L./Dunbar, I.
Attraction of beagles to conspecific urine,
vaginal and anal secretion odors
Physiology and Behaviour, Vol. 12, 825-833, 1974

Evans, Howard E.
Miller's anatomy of the dog
Saunders (WB) Co Ltd 1993

Frings, S.
Chemoelectrical signal transduction in olfactory
sensory neurons of air-breathing vertebrates
Cellular and Molecular Life Sciences 58, 510-519,
2001

Good, P.R. et al.
The effect of oestrogen on odour detection
chemical senses and flavour, 2, 45-48, 1976

Goody, Peter
Dog anatomy: A pictorial approach to canine
structure
J A Allen & Co Limited 1998

Guttridge, N.M.
Changes in ocular and visual variables during
the menstrual cycle
Ophthal. Physiol. Opt. 14. 38-48, 1994

Horgan, J.
See spot see blue: curb the dogma!
Canines are not colour-blind
Scientific American, 262, 20, 1990

Kobal, G. et al
Is there directional smelling?
Experientia. 45, 130-134, 1989

Lippincott, Williams and Wilkins
Dog breeds: an illustrated guide
Anatomical Chart Company 2002

McConnell, P.B.
Acoustic structure and receiver response in
domestic dogs, canis familiaris
Anim. Behav. 39, 897-904, 1990

McConnell, P.B./Baylis, J.R.
Interspecific communication in cooperative herding:
Acoustic and visual signals from human shepherds
and herding dogs
Z. Tierpsychologie, 67, 302-328, 1985

McDowell, Lyon
The dog in action
Dogwise Publishing 2002

Morin, L.P.
The circadian visual system
Brain Research Reviews 67, 102-127, 1994

Moulton, D.G./Beidler, L.M.
Structure and function in the peripheral
olfactory system
Physiological Reviews, 7, 1-52, 1967

Moulton, D.G./Marshall, D.A.
The performance of dogs in detecting –
Ionone in the vapor phase
J. comp. Physiol. 110, 287-306, 1976

Neitz, M./Neitz, J.
Molecular genetics and the biological basis
of colour vision
In: Backhaus, W.G.K./Kliegel, R./Werner, J.S.:
Colour Vision. de Gruyter Berlin 1998

Pickles, J.O.
An introduction to the physiology of hearing
Academic Press, 1982

Price, S.
Mechanisms of stimulation of olfactory neurons: An
essay
Ann. NY Acad. Sci., 341-354, 1983

Ressler, K.J./Sullivan, S.L./Buck, L.B.
A molecular dissection of spatial patterning
in the olfactory system
Current Opinion in Neurobiology 4, 588-596, 1994

Robinson, Roy
Genetics for dog breeders
Pergamon Press, 1990

Walker, J.C. et al
Olfactory and trigeminal response of nicotine
Drug Development Research, 38, 160-168